Analysis of teaching physical education

?

1995

Analysis of teaching
PHYSICAL EDUCATION

WILLIAM G. ANDERSON, Ed.D.

Teachers College, Columbia University,
New York, New York

Illustrated

The C. V. Mosby Company

ST. LOUIS • TORONTO • LONDON   1980

The C. V. Mosby Company
11830 Westline Industrial Drive, St. Louis, Missouri 63141

Library of Congress Cataloging in Publication Data

Anderson, William G
  Analysis of teaching physical education.

  Includes bibliographical references and index.
    1. Physical education and training—Study and teach-
ing. 2. Observation (Educational method) I. Title.
GV362.A5   613.7′07   79-20074
ISBN 0-8016-0179-7

VT/M/M   9 8 7 6 5 4 3 2 1   01/D/077

To
RAYLA

Foreword

This book represents a bridge between research and practice. Presented here are new instruments and techniques for observing and analyzing the teaching of physical education. Both the tools and the procedures are the end products of a planned sequence of investigations that began more than a decade ago. The first published account of the use of systematic observation to study life in the gymnasium appeared in 1967. By that date, the author and his associates at Teachers College already were at work designing instruments and gathering data about the behaviors of teachers and students in physical education.

Bill Anderson had been quick to realize the potential significance of the research establishment's new interest in classroom observation systems—the "shot-charts" of investigations performed in natural school settings. Although he had some initial reservations about the utility of descriptive analytic research for any immediate improvement of teaching practice and teacher training, Anderson understood the sequence of events that would be necessary to reach that goal. First would come instrument development, then the accumulation of a broad data base, next careful description of the real world, and, finally, application to teaching and teacher education.

Over more than a decade, the Teachers College group has diligently worked its way through the first three stages of this scenario. The discovery that individual teachers can make direct use of observation instruments for the purpose of improving instruction now has led Anderson to move on to the final stage of the projected sequence. In this book he shifts from the role of describer to the role of improver and attends directly to the problems of teachers and teacher educators.

Some purists will complain that in the absence of complete understanding of all factors involved in teaching motor skills, we should not dare to suggest improvement through self-analysis. A completely verified theory of teaching would indeed be useful, but we do not have one now. More importantly, given the complexity of events in the gym, we are not likely to achieve a research-based model within our lifetime.

Anderson's faith throughout this long project has been that once the profession and, more importantly, individual teachers were aware of what really happens in physical education classes, they would act intelligently to adjust and improve what they do. Field tests of the materials in this book confirm that faith and fully justify the decision to proceed now rather than wait for the slow grinding of our research machinery to produce perfect prescriptions for practice.

Presently, most physical education teachers are neither encouraged to struggle with the problem of improving instruction nor equipped with any reliable form of feedback for their efforts. A format through which teachers can gather data from their own classes for use in self-analysis and improvement offers rewards that easily outweigh the risks inherent in working with aspects of instruction not yet perfectly understood.

The cautious discipline and unassuming dignity of the author's style will at first hide the fact that this book foments revolution in the gym. Use and close acquaintance, however, will betray the book's true purposes—to encourage teachers to believe what they thought impossible, to do what they thought inappropriate, and to exercise powers of decision and control they thought beyond their capacity. The majority of physical education teachers do not believe it possible to subject the act of instruction to empirical analysis, do not think it safe and appropriate to share the task of improving instructional skills with colleagues, and accept it as their lot to struggle fitfully and often ineffectively to exert deliberate and systematic control over their teaching behaviors. This text, disguised as an innocent-appearing teacher workbook, is a revolutionary tract thrown over the fortress walls at night, intended to encourage desertion from those self-destructive beliefs.

The use of systems for direct observation of teaching and the gathering of low-inference behavioral data break with a long history of treating the gym as a black box. Teachers, students, hardware, curriculum content, and organization have been fed into one end and various consequences observed at the other. It often has been assumed that the process events that go on inside the class, the acts of teaching and learning, could be ignored as either irrelevant or not amenable to the processes of empirical science. This attitude has proved disabling to research and practice alike. Neither in training nor in daily practice have teachers been encouraged to look at teaching as a series of observable and knowable events. Only the rhetoric of grand objectives, the skinny outlines of theoretical models, and the ubiquitous exhortation to "do it good" have been available to guide teachers as they grappled with the problems of instruction.

The use of teacher teams to provide mutual assistance and support in the process of self-analysis also breaks sharply with the traditions of the school. Ethnographic studies reveal that teachers work in a remarkable degree of isolation from each other. Visiting another teacher's class is a rare event and cooperative enterprise to improve teaching skills would be unthinkable in many schools. Many of the procedures presented in this book demand that teachers work together. Such joint participation in clinical tasks will erode the egg carton structure that isolates teachers both during training and on the job. Although it may not have been so intended by the author, the careful definition of functions provided for each cooperative task will work to protect student peers and teacher colleagues as they learn to play new, interactive role behaviors.

Finally, the book makes explicit use of certain powerful expectations about teachers, all of which run counter to an implicit set of beliefs that prevail in physical education. Teaching is treated as though it were a complex orchestration of skills that requires constant and sometimes heroic efforts to master. Teachers (the readers) are treated as though they must make difficult decisions about this complex process, must think reflectively about the meaning of empirical evidence, and must learn how to use instruments and rational processes to seek improvement. Expectations do exert a powerful influence on human behavior. In that fact we may find an explanation for why field trials found teachers so responsive and competent in their use of the processes contained in this book.

The author's own evident values will make it easier for many readers to accept so many violations of traditional belief. The tone of hard-headed practicality will appeal to all who have to confront the difficult realities of life in the gymnasium. That tone is perfectly matched to present-day attitudes among teachers—particularly among young physical educators. There is an implicit kind of stern morality here; "teaching makes a difference and you are accountable for doing it well!" This is mixed, however, with healthy doses of skepticism about superficial maxims and simplistic notions concerning the evaluation of teacher performance.

The vast majority of physical education teachers want to do their work better. Where there is credible hope of improving their skills, they will risk both personal investment and all sorts of institutional and collegial sanctions. This is precisely the attraction that Anderson extends to his readers: a believable chance to improve the quality of what happens in the gym. No easy prescriptions here; just a workable process, a challenge, and a vision.

Lawrence F. Locke

Professor of Education and Physical Education
The University of Massachusetts

Preface

The analysis of teaching is a comparatively new area of study within teacher education—new enough, in fact, to be greeted by many educators with a certain amount of perplexity and even skepticism. In the past, teacher preparation programs have stressed knowledge of subject matter and skill in executing teaching methods. Training in the analysis of what happens when one teaches has been incidental at best, and often entirely neglected.

Today there is a growing emphasis on preparing teachers to analyze what happens in their classes. A variety of systematic techniques is used to collect information about classroom events, and the information obtained is used to plan and execute needed changes. This emphasis on analysis has been spawned, in part, by recent research on teaching that yielded valuable techniques for studying real-world events in the classroom or gymnasium and produced surprising, sometimes shocking, accounts of what actually happens in class. The emphasis was given further impetus when teacher educators discovered that, given the appropriate tools for analyzing what happens in their classes, teachers are capable of making enormous improvements in their own performance—and can do so largely on their own. Foremost, however, increased attention to the analysis of teaching has been fueled by the recognition that preparation in systematic analysis is crucial to continued professional growth; teachers equipped with the tools for analyzing what they do are in a position to guide their own future development.

This text deals with the analysis of teaching in physical education. It provides teachers with opportunities to develop skills in analyzing what happens in their classes. Many of the analytic techniques used have grown out of descriptive-analytic studies of physical education classes conducted at Teachers College, Columbia University during the past 10 years. All of the techniques have been field tested by preservice and inservice teachers and then revised to make them more suitable for use in a variety of school settings. More than fifty teachers participated in the field testing.

To use this text effectively you should be actively engaged in teaching physical education, either as a student teacher or as a regularly employed teacher. You will be asked to complete a series of Clinical Tasks that involve teaching classes and analyzing what happens in classes. Most of the analyses will be done in relation to your own teaching; some of it will involve analyzing classes taught by others. Since, in several instances, data on what happens in your classes will have to be collected by someone else while you teach, it will be important for you to have a collaborator. If you are an employed teacher, try to enlist the cooperation of a colleague or supervisor. If you are a student teacher, your cooperating teacher, college supervisor, or a fellow student teacher can work with you.

Our field tests suggest that practice in the analysis of teaching is profitable to both experienced and novice teachers. In fact I've been astonished by the apparent value derived by experienced teachers—whom I previously thought would resist self-analysis and change. Quite the opposite, they seem to appreciate the added insights into "what I've been doing all these years." On the other hand, novice teachers should not get deeply involved in the analysis of their own teaching at too early a point. They need time to gain some confidence and adopt a comfortable style of teaching before they begin to scrutinize their own performance. So, work in the analysis of teaching should come toward the middle or later stages of the student teaching experience. However, at an early stage of their training, student teachers may profit from analyzing classes taught by their cooperating teacher.

I owe a great deal to the more than fifty teachers who field tested the materials in this text. Their feedback helped me to cut out the superfluous, clarify the vague, expand the useful, redirect the errant, and ensure the practicability of the whole enterprise.

I am also indebted to the researchers who worked with me during the past 10 years in studying teaching in physical education classes. Special thanks go to the members of the Data Bank Project: Gary Barrette, Linda Catelli, John Costello, Rachelle Goldsmith, Richard Hurwitz, Sue Kelly, Edward Kennedy, Susan Laubach, Mitchell Levison, Bruce Morgenegg, Charles Tobey, and LeRoy Weisberg; and to Sylvia Fishman. Their creative ideas have added immeasurably to my understanding of teaching.

Thanks are also due Shirley Cooper, Ph.D., John Fowler, Ph.D., and Robert Pestolesi, Ph.D., publishers's reviewers, for their comments and recommendations.

William G. Anderson

Note to the instructor using this text in a course

This book is designed for use as a text in an undergraduate course in student teaching or methods of teaching or in a graduate course in the analysis of teaching. It should be used flexibly. Although I have tried to arrange the chapters and tasks in a logical sequence and to incorporate a comprehensive array of analytic techniques, the order and contents are not sacrosanct. Feel free to revise the order, to delete Tasks, to add others, or to revise existing Tasks. The intent should be to provide *your* students with a solid grounding in the analysis of teaching; be as selective as you need to be in achieving that goal.

The Clinical Tasks are designed to be carried out in a field setting by the teachers (or student teachers) enrolled in your course. In this setting they work in collaboration with a colleague or cooperating teacher; you need not be there (although it might be nice to visit the school on occasion). You can monitor their work by examining the completed clinical records and discussing them with the teachers.

Teachers who go through this process of analysis need someone to talk to about their findings. Hopefully they can talk to their collaborators in the field. In addition, you can help by providing for small-group seminars where teachers can compare notes and share ideas, or by making yourself available for consultation.

While all of the Clinical Tasks can be completed using live observation, a few can be done more effectively by using videotaped recordings. This procedure allows teachers to observe their own performances (on tape) and complete detailed analyses from a variety of perspectives. If you can possibly arrange for each of the teachers in your class to be videotaped at least once, it would add immeasurably to the experience.

This book can be read in a few hours, but to complete the Clinical Tasks properly requires substantial amounts of time, so be reasonable in making assignments and setting deadlines. Our experience indicates that most full-time, in-service teachers require a full semester to complete all of the Tasks—some take longer. Student teachers may be able to complete only 60% or 70% of the

Tasks in a semester, depending on their other assignments and responsibilities. In any event, the teachers should be allowed to work on the Tasks at their own pace; don't expect everyone to complete the same task at the same time. The ultimate goal of this whole enterprise is not to complete the Tasks; it's to become a skilled analyst of one's own teaching.

Contents

Analysis of teaching physical education

Introduction

Teachers operate in an immensely complicated and demanding world. They face thirty or more students at once—each one different from the other, demanding individualized attention and treatment. They must respond to a continuous and rapid succession of events, many of which are unanticipated, leaving little time for thoughtful decision-making. Teaching situations change from moment to moment; no two are ever quite the same. Yesterday's solution is today's blunder. Confronted with this sort of turmoil, teachers are supposed to accomplish an imposing array of goals; some of which are concrete, others esoteric, none easily achieved. Little wonder that novice teachers are overwhelmed by what they encounter.

Of course we prepare teachers to cope with these complex realities. They are schooled in subject matter, imbued with an understanding of student characteristics, trained in the use of various instructional methods, and so on. The preparation is consummated by providing opportunities to plan lessons and to practice teach, all of which we hope will enable prospective teachers to launch their careers in appropriate fashion. We have no illusions, however, that their preparation is complete; a lot remains to be learned "on the job." As they encounter new situations, deal with different students, experiment with new techniques, teachers will continue to learn and, we hope, improve; experience, we assume, is a most powerful teacher of teachers.

Not everyone, however, profits equally well from experience. Some people claim they never make the same mistake twice. They are the exceptions. (Exceptions in the sense that they are extraordinarily able to capitalize on past experience, or are extraordinarily extravagant in their claims.) Most of us correct some mistakes, but repeat others. Some of us apparently profit very little from past experience. Consider the teacher in a rut who does the same thing day after day, week after week, year in and year out. The absence of change normally signals the inability to profit from experience.

Failure to learn from experience may have several origins. The teacher's day is so crowded with events and responsibilities that there may be no time to reflect on

1

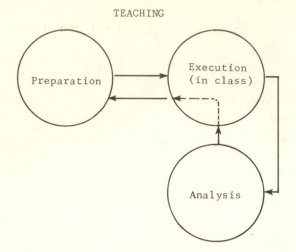

what has happened. Recognizing the complexity of classroom events, some teachers have difficulty sorting out and interpreting what occurred. Others are just too lazy to bother. In part the inability to profit from experience may be traced to teacher education programs that train teachers to plan lessons and teach, but not to analyze and evaluate what transpires during class. In effect teachers are trained to *do,* but not to *figure out* what happened. Instead, assessment is left to the supervisor or cooperating teacher. Not surprisingly, the graduates of such programs have neither the inclination nor the skills required to analyze their own teaching.

This brings us to the major premise of this book: *In order to profit from your experience in teaching and so to continue to develop competence in teaching, you should develop skill in the analysis of teaching.*

This premise is based on a concept of teaching that includes the analysis of past events as an *integral part* of the teaching process. Analysis of teaching is not a convenient adjunct to teaching; it *is* teaching. (See figure above.)

Let me go a step further and suggest that your analysis of what happened in class is as important as what you actually do in class. Outlandish? I think not. Failure to analyze teaching and use it as a basis for change leads to stagnation. Inept analysis leads to misdirected development.

THE ANALYSIS OF TEACHING

Basically, the analysis of teaching involves: observing what happens during class, compiling a record of those observations, interpreting and/or evaluating the record, and making decisions about the needed changes in future classes.

Left to our own devices, we adopt *personal styles* of analysis that tend to be informal, subjective, and stereotypical. That is, we usually make *mental notes* based on casual recollections; our personal biases influence what we perceive and how we interpret those perceptions; and we normally focus on the same kind of events from one class to the next. Such idiosyncratic methods of analysis are useful, but limited. Consider, for example, the teachers who constantly reflect on their own behavior but are relatively oblivious to the nuances of student behavior, or the teachers whose subjective impressions are never modified by access to more objective evidence, or the teachers who are so preoccupied with student involvement that they neglect to appraise student learning.

If teaching were simple, the analysis of teaching would be simple. No training in analysis would be required; our personal approaches would suffice. Teaching is not simple; neither is analysis. No one analytic method can even begin to account for the multitude of things that happen in a class—distinct methods with different foci are needed. All techniques for collecting information about teaching (whether informal or "scientific") are limited in terms of the validity, scope, and utility of the data they yield. Various data collection techniques have to be employed to produce a reasonably balanced and comprehensive picture of what happens.

This text is designed to expose you to an array of methods for analyzing teaching. You will employ methods that:

1. *Focus on different targets:* Student behavior, teacher behavior, teacher-student interaction, student learning.
2. *Use different observers/evaluators:* The teacher, a colleague, a supervisor, students.
3. *Involve various techniques for collecting data:* Informal notes, descriptive codings of events, criterion-referenced ratings, subjective/narrative reports, test scores.
4. *Record different dimensions of teaching:* Student involvement in activities, student practice, student progress, student affective responses, teacher roles, teacher's method of communication, lesson content, the manner of teacher-student interaction, and several others.

Skillful use of these methods is developed by completing an extensive series of *clinical tasks,* twenty in all. Each task involves the analysis of actual events in teaching. In most instances the analysis will be of your own teaching—on occasion you will observe classes taught by others. As with other teaching skills, analytic skills are developed through application and practice. Expect to spend a considerable amount of time observing teaching, actually teaching, and interpreting records of teaching. If all you have time for is to *read* this text, forget about it—it's not worth it.

Beyond merely using these methods you will learn their characteristic strengths, weaknesses, limitations, and the purposes for which each approach is best suited. Some methods yield objective and reliable data; others are more subjective and less reliable. Some deal only in quantities, others in qualities. Some observational techniques are flexible, others are highly structured. Some approaches monitor overt behavior, others get at more covert phenomena. Some are appropriate for measuring the means of instruction, others for measuring the outcomes of instruction. Some take into account the teacher's own intentions and goals, others do not. Familiarity with these characteristics should enable you to use the methods intelligently in the future.

The analytic methods have been selected, in part, as a consequence of years of research in the analysis of teaching (Anderson and Barrette, 1978). Sophisticated analytic systems developed for use in research in physical education (Anderson, 1974; Fishman, 1974; Laubach, 1975; Morgenegg, 1977) provided some of the ideas on which the methods were formulated. Other research and authoritative writing on classroom interaction (see References) were also helpful. Extensive field tests of each clinical task played a pivotal role in the ultimate selection of methods. Experienced and prospective physical education teachers completed the tasks in school settings and provided feedback that was used to add, delete, and revise methods. Many decisions were made on very pragmatic grounds: Could teachers use the method? Did it yield information that they considered valuable?

Don't be misled by this buildup. You will not know all there is to know about the analysis of teaching upon completing this book. The field is in its infancy, as is my knowledge of it.

What can you expect to achieve as a result of completing the clinical tasks? First, you can expect to come away with a set of skills that can be used as tools in your future work in teaching, tools that can be selected, or combined, or reshaped to suit *your own* ends, to fit *your* teaching situation, to gauge progress toward *your* goals. Second, you will be aware of many facets of teaching that heretofore had not entered your mind. This heightened awareness will yield heightened understanding—not that you will have a firm grasp of all the constituents of teaching, but you will better appreciate the nature of some of those constituents. Finally, you should improve your teaching.

ON IMPROVING TEACHING

While the principal focus of this text is on the development of skill in using analytic techniques, in the process you will collect an enormous amount of information about your own teaching. Furthermore, at each step in the process, you will evaluate that teaching and decide what, if anything, needs to be changed. Then, whenever possible, you will make the changes in a subsequent class. If the analyses are rigorously done, you can expect to make a lot of changes (at least that was the experience of most teachers in the field tests). If the analyses are intelligently done, you can expect the changes to constitute improvements.

But improvements by whose standards? Primarily by your own standards, or possibly by a colleague's standards, a supervisor's standards, or your students' standards. Certainly *not* by my standards. I don't know your teaching situation, or your goals, or what you've tried before, or your style of teaching, or the peculiarities of your students. So don't expect patented prescriptions for how to teach in the chapters ahead. (Frankly, I never have been able to locate a prescription that I was confident enough in to recommend to everyone.) You are going to have to decide what's good or bad, what should be changed, and whether the changes were better than what went before.

This is an uncomfortable task for many teachers, especially those who have been trained to rely on the judgments of professors, or supervisors, or textbook writers to tell them whether their performance is up to par. By all means do seek advice from others; do use the things you've learned from texts, teachers, and other sources to *support* your evaluations; but let the final judgments be mainly your own.

1

Informal analysis

Most professional observation and analysis of teaching are done informally. Observers simply "sit in on a class" and watch what goes on. There is no advance planning. They carry no rating scales or coding forms. They see what they choose to see from their own professional viewpoint and remember (or record) the things that strike them as significant. Student teachers, for example, spend much of their time informally observing cooperating teachers; novice teachers learn the ropes by informally watching their experienced colleagues; department chairmen and supervisors often "drop in" to see how things are going. Indeed, the careers of most experienced professionals are replete with hundreds or even thousands of hours of informal observation and analysis.

Unquestionably this form of observation and analysis has a profound impact on professional thought and practice. Our sense of what's going on in our field is shaped by it. Our conception of effective and ineffective practices as well as our notions about needed improvements stem primarily from such observations.

When informal analysis is viewed as including self-analysis—those occasions when we casually recollect what happened in our own classes—its significance looms even larger. Most of our decisions about how to improve our teaching hinge on informal perceptions of what happened last period, or yesterday, or last semester. Indeed, our very growth as professionals over the years is contingent upon the persistence and quality of our attempts at informal self-analysis.

Given the likelihood that most of your past and future analyses of teaching have been, and will be, of the informal variety, it seems appropriate to start this consideration of various analytic approaches by first concentrating on *informal analysis*. This will provide you with an opportunity to reexamine your normal mode of looking at teaching, identify some of its distinctive characteristics, and provide a jumping-off point for subsequent explorations of other approaches.

BEFORE READING ANY FURTHER, PLEASE COMPLETE CLINICAL TASK 1 AND, IF POSSIBLE, CLINICAL TASK 2.

Clinical Task 1—INFORMAL PROFESSIONAL ANALYSIS

Informally observe a physical education class (not your own), preferably an entire class, or perhaps a few 10- or 20-minute segments of different classes. Keep notes on what happened—be sure to include the most important aspects of the class.

If possible, have a colleague observe and take notes on the same class so that you can compare and discuss observations afterward.

Clinical Task 2—INFORMAL SELF-ANALYSIS

Use *informal professional analysis* to record and analyze a sample of your own teaching. Immediately after you have taught a class, use informal notes to record what happened—be sure to include the most important aspects of the class.

If possible, have a colleague (or cooperating teacher, or supervisor) observe and take notes on the same class so that you can compare and discuss observations afterward.

I've asked you not to read beyond this point until you've completed Tasks 1 and 2 so that your informal analysis will be spontaneous and natural. If you read about the "characteristics of informal analysis" before completing the tasks, it will distort your natural tendencies and the whole experience will be a flop.

CHARACTERISTICS OF INFORMAL ANALYSIS

Although informal analyses differ substantially from one another in form, content, and quality, most of these analyses share certain common characteristics, some of which are discussed briefly here. It should be interesting to examine the extent to which your own informal analyses (Tasks 1 and 2) contain these common characteristics.

To provide additional perspective, three informal analyses appear on p. 8. They were completed by three experienced physical educators, all of whom observed the *same* class, and all of whom were given the same instructions you were (see Task 1).

A small piece of the action

Your analyses (as well as those on p. 8) succeeded in capturing only a small part of what happened. In the face of numerous concurrent events, you saw and heard only one at a time. Further, you were able to recollect and/or record only a small part of what you saw and heard.

Think for a moment about the fragmentary nature of your notes and recollections in comparison to the rich and complete network of interconnecting events that actually transpired in reality. In fact, if the lesson you observed was on

SAMPLE INFORMAL ANALYSES

These informal notes are based on observation of the first 20
minutes of a fourth grade class. The class started with warm-up
exercises and then participated in parachute activities.

Observer 1

-very structured
-can't hear directions for
 exercises
-no individualization
-no comments on individual
 performances
-exceedingly long warm-up
 time
-little interaction be-
 tween teacher and stu-
 dents
-reinforcing comments
 were superficial
-well organized
-good directions for
 organization
-took time to explain
 basic concepts
-no required uniforms
-teacher didn't seem to
 know students by names

Observer 2

-students were rushed
 through the calisthenics,
 the teacher placed no
 emphasis on the proper
 form of the exercises
-boys and girls were di-
 vided to play separately
-teacher said, "If you are
 good you'll get picked"
-teacher posed useful questions that helped students
 understand how the para-
 chute behaves and how it
 can be manipulated
-the teaching was extremely
 structured which contributed to class control

Observer 3

-teacher efficiently
 organizes class for
 warm-ups (one minute)
-exercises are unre-
 lated to main activity
-keeps saying "nice job,
 nice job," over and over
-his attitude toward stu-
 dents is condescending
-had boys choose teams,
 criticized girls (sex
 discrimination)
-teacher used "command
 teaching" rather than
 asking thinking questions
 and having children
 think out their answers
-I think this teacher is
 an exparatrooper

videotape and you observed it again on two or three occasions, you would be surprised to discover the number of new things you see with each review.

Of course the fragmentary nature of observation and analysis is not unique to the informal approach. *All forms* of observation and analysis of teaching are, by necessity, fragmentary. None of them begins to capture the full reality of a gymnasium in which thirty or more human beings continually interact. This fact should become more and more evident as we proceed through the analytic tasks contained in the remainder of this book.

A personal perspective

Much of your record of events was determined by what actually happened—i.e., the occurrence of the event dictated your recording of it and your reaction to it. In another sense, however, you did *choose* to record some happenings and not others, to make some evaluative judgments and not others, and to describe those happenings and judgments in a particular way. In all likelihood, many of your choices were based on your own concept of teaching—i.e., those aspects of teaching that you have come to believe are most crucial. For example, you may have noted the affective tone of the teacher's interaction with students ("supportive," "positive," "harsh," or "critical") because of the importance you attribute to this dimension of classroom climate, or you may have noted the prevailing skill practice conditions ("inadequate number of practice trials for students," "teacher gave frequent corrective feedback," etc.) because you believe the facilitation of skill acquisition is one of the teacher's principal roles; and so on.

Thus the focal points for informal analysis are in large part subjectively determined. It should not surprise you then that the points emphasized in one informal analysis will differ from those emphasized in another, even when the analyses pertain to the same lesson. Compare the analyses on p. 8; all three observers analyzed the same class. If a colleague observed the same class you did (Task 1), compare your observations.

Focus on the teacher

When done by professionals, informal analyses have a tendency to focus on the actions of the teacher, or on the interactions between the teacher and selected students. Perhaps this is because, as professionals, we empathize more readily with the teacher; or perhaps it's a function of the dominant role that so many teachers play in most classes. In any event the teacher normally gets a disproportionate share of our attention, given the fact that he or she is only one of thirty or more important human beings in the educational setting.

Of course we also watch individual students when for one reason or another they attract our attention. But more often than not, we come away with a general impression of what "most of the students" were doing at various points in time.

An inclination to evaluate

Most informal observers have a propensity for making immediate value judgments about what they see. (Notice the numerous judgments in the analyses on p. 8, and, perhaps, in your own record—despite the fact that you were instructed only to "observe" and "keep notes on what happened.") When left to their own devices, professional observers have a natural tendency to describe things in terms of how well they are working, or whether the teacher is doing the right thing. Indeed, in many instances, the informal record is a chronicle of the things the teacher didn't do, or events that should have but didn't occur. It's as though the professional observer, immediately upon encountering a class, constructs a set of expectations about what *should happen*, and thereafter fixates on whether or not these expectations are fulfilled.

Self-analysis: intentions, thoughts, and reality

If you had an opportunity to complete an informal self-analysis (Task 2) you should find that many of the preceding characteristics apply equally well to that self-analysis. In addition, your self-analysis is likely to focus on the match between your intentions and what happened in reality. If your plan for the class centered on providing a good skill demonstration or on handling a certain kind of behavioral problem that frequently arose in the class, the chances are that your recollections and record would account for whether these plans were fulfilled. Or, at any moment, if you were trying to do something that didn't pan out (such as get the students' attention, or spend more time with Jane, who needed your help), you are likely to remember these momentary discrepancies between intentions and actions.

Also, your self-analytic record is likely to contain some references to your thoughts and feelings during the class. Perhaps you "couldn't think of that student's name" or you "got angry at Johnny for not paying attention."

If you were fortunate enough to have a colleague observe your class (Task 2) and he was not privy to your plans, in all likelihood his record does not focus on the important elements of your plan. Furthermore, his perceptions and recollections are likely to account for none of your thoughts and feelings.

The enduring record

A few weeks or months after the observation and analysis, the only real enduring record of what happened in the class is the written words and the associated memories they conjure up—most other recollections fade.

The informal record is likely to have personal meaning for the observer since it focuses on events that are important to him, and uses his own best terms to describe those events. On the other hand, the words used to describe events have no agreed-upon or standardized definitions. So, for instance, an entry indicating that the teacher "disciplined" a student may have meant one thing to the observer and may mean something quite different to someone else who tries to interpret the record. Indeed, the observer's conception of what "discipline" means may change over time, and thus his own interpretation of the record may change in retrospect.

Furthermore, the method of informal observation is not bound by any rules. And so, among other things, the scope and context of the record are not discernible. For example, a record might indicate that "the teacher didn't interact with individual students." Since we don't know the method of observation that was used, we have no way of knowing whether the entry was based on one incident or many, whether the teacher didn't interact with individuals on 80%, 90%, or 100% of the observed occasions, or indeed whether the observer kept any sort of continuous count of the type of teacher-student interaction. Hence we know very little about the raw data on which the entry was based.

INFORMAL ANALYSIS: AN ASSESSMENT

By this time, you may have concluded that I don't think too highly of informal analysis. Please don't. Informal analysis has been, is, and will continue to be the predominant approach to analyzing teaching. This is as it should be.

As a responsible, independent professional, you must be free to encounter teaching from your *own* perspective, focus on things that *you* feel are important, evaluate events using *your own* criteria for good teaching, and use *your own* judgment to isolate critical problems and suggest solutions. It's through such experiences that the analysis of teaching takes on personal meaning—you come to learn better what you value, where you stand, and what you know you should do. On the contrary, to be continuously constrained to use someone else's rating scale, or check list, or coding system, is an exercise in self-denial.

Another virtue of informal analysis is that it leaves you free to react spontaneously to significant but unforeseen events. When those decisive events occur (i.e., the teacher seizes on a teachable moment, or reacts humanely to a distraught student, or loses control of the class, etc.), you can dwell on them, examine and reexamine them, and forget about the surrounding trivia. In contrast, a carefully planned analysis sometimes precludes the consideration of such events by coercing us into rating or coding prescribed events at fixed intervals—with the result that our record often misses the forest for the trees.

Yet, as you engage in informal analysis, recognize it for what it is—don't operate under the impression that you are doing something you're not. Recognize that it is subjective and not objective; i.e., you see what you choose to see and judge things as you choose to judge them, which is not the same as others see them or judge them. Realize that your observations lack reliability in the sense that what you saw on one occasion is not the same as what you would see if given an opportunity to reobserve the same class. Understand that your record is fragmentary, not comprehensive, and is subject to various interpretations. And finally, recognize that you may have jumped into making value judgments without fully appreciating the teacher's intentions and the past history of the class, and without being keenly aware of the data on which your judgments are based.

The value of any approach to the analysis of teaching has to be gauged in relation to the purpose for which it is used, and its appropriateness compared to other approaches available for accomplishing the same purpose. Informal analysis is no exception. It effectively accomplishes some purposes, but is comparatively inappropriate for accomplishing others, for example:

Informal analysis of selected problem areas in an inexperienced colleague's teaching performance may be the only way to get at the solution to those problems and at the same time maintain a friendship.

Informal analysis and evaluation of a teacher's performance, when that analysis will be used to make decisions about the teacher's tenure or retention on the staff, is likely to be grossly arbitrary and unfair.

In many circumstances, informal self-analysis may be the only practicable approach to collecting information for use in making day-to-day decisions about alterations in teaching strategies.

I pity the poor student teacher whose supervisor relies primarily on informal analysis to evaluate performance—especially when the supervisor's personal criteria are not known to the student teacher in advance.

I feel sorry for the teacher who, when asked to produce evidence of accountability to the school board, is forced to report informal subjective impressions of how well students are progressing.

MAKING CHANGES

The ultimate reason for engaging in most analyses of teaching is to improve teaching. To complete an analysis and then simply file it away is an unconscionable waste of time. Clinical Task 3 encourages you to use the informal analysis of your teaching (Task 2) as a basis for deciding on and instituting improvements.

Clinical Task 3—USING INFORMAL ANALYSIS AS A BASIS FOR CHANGING TEACHING

Using your own and/or an observer's analysis of your teaching (Task 2):

1. Review the record yourself, or together with the observer, and ask yourself:
   a. What changes would yield improvement? (Compose list.)
   b. Which of these changes are immediately feasible?
   c. Which *one* or *two* of the feasible changes are most important?
2. Write out the changes identified in *c* above; include a brief description of any actions you will have to take as a teacher to implement these changes.
3. Reteach the lesson or a similar lesson concentrating on the intended changes.
4. If possible, have a colleague watch you reteach the lesson, concentrating on whether you successfully institute the change. Otherwise, take notes yourself, immediately after the class, indicating whether or not you made the changes.
5. Discuss the results with your observer or another colleague.

The first step in the procedures outlined in Task 3 is to examine the informal analytic record and identify needed changes. In most instances, the record will contain evaluative judgments that imply logical changes. If not, you will have to use the record to jog your memory with respect to needed changes. In either case, recognize that while an identified problem or deficiency may suggest the direction for the needed change, there are usually several alternative ways of correcting the problem. Survey the alternative corrective actions before choosing the one you will pursue.

If you can find no needed changes, fine. Perhaps it was a very good class. How about analyzing another one or two or three of your classes until you find something that needs improvement? If you do so, and still can't locate any needed improvements, hurry back to the bookstore and try to get a refund on this book.

Step *1b* of the procedures suggests that you identify changes that are *immediately feasible*. This refers to the kinds of changes that could be readily made in a subsequent reteach lesson, such as changes in methodology, class organization, arrangement of equipment, etc. It is entirely possible that your analytic record will also point to the need for other kinds of changes that require longer term solutions such as insufficient equipment, overcrowded class, and so on. Needless to say, these may be important problems and should be attended to. For now, however, don't let these long-term problems deter you from making immediately feasible changes.

The procedures also suggest that you isolate *one* or *two* changes. Our experience indicates that it is difficult for teachers to concentrate on making more than two kinds of changes at once—especially when those changes represent departures from normal routines or behavioral patterns. Furthermore, concentrating on one or two changes allows you to analyze the execution of each change more thoroughly. Of course, if you have identified several needed changes and find it difficult to isolate one or two that are more important than others, there is nothing to stop you from doing several reteach lessons, concentrating on a different change in each one.

A move toward structure

At this point be aware of the fact that the analysis of the reteach lesson is more structured than your initial analysis (Tasks 1 and 2). You have *planned* the observation. Both the observation and analysis have a focus, the intended changes. What you have done is to move one step away from the completely informal approach, which was devoid of preplanning and preestablished focus. You are no longer free to look for whatever you choose; you've made a prior commitment to search out preselected events. Realize that, as a result of this structure, you will probably see those events more clearly and overlook other events not within the focus.

INFORMAL ANALYSIS BY STUDENTS

Up to this point, we have concentrated on informal *professional* analysis— i.e., analysis done by trained teachers—which tends to focus on features of classes that have natural interest and value for professionals. There is another potentially valuable source of feedback about teaching—the students. They can provide a somewhat different and yet remarkably insightful appraisal of classroom events. After all, *they* are the people for whom the whole educational process is designed and it is the nature of *their* experiences that determines the success or failure of that process. It stands to reason that they are in a unique position to provide useful information about those experiences.

Consider the following excerpts from evaluations that were solicited from students in physical education classes. They constitute a very small, and not particularly representative, sample of the comments we have collected from several different schools and grade levels—third through twelfth.

I didn't like the races because I've done a lot of it and it's kind of boring if you're never a winner.

The best thing about today's class was wrestling Adler. I always wanted to kill him.

I wish you would stop all the bull (meaning instruction) so we could play more.

I liked playing the game much better than I liked the drills, but I know you wouldn't be able to do it without drills. So I suppose having the drills should be liked just as much as playing the game. So I liked them both.

Stop picking on me.

Our teacher is nice because she is fair.

I didn't like playing crab soccer because the floor was too dirty.

I think we are always learning things that we already know. It's a waste of time.

I don't like when people cheat and move into somebody else's position when the person who was there can do the job fine.

The class was fun today, I guess because everybody was friends and nobody got into fights; you know, just fooling around.

I don't like gymnastics sometimes because I can hurt myself sometimes.

It's embarrassing because I can't do it and everyone else is really good.

I hate basketball. The only good thing about basketball is hitting some chick (Patty Morgan) with the basketball.

Despite the logic of seeking out student input on teaching, it seems to be done very rarely. During my observations of and contacts with hundreds of experienced physical education teachers over the past few years, virtually none has sought student opinions or judgments in any systematic or regular way. The only student input that does seem to surface with any degree of regularity is the occasional "complaint" lodged by the student who is courageous enough to register it.

So, at this point, I'm going to suggest that you provide an opportunity for the students in a class you are teaching to informally analyze that class. The method of collecting the information and the form in which it appears are not crucial, provided the students have a legitimate opportunity to choose the aspects of the class *they* feel are most important and describe or judge them in ways *they* feel are most appropriate. Try to give the students as much freedom as you had in conducting your informal analysis. Clinical Task 4 outlines the general steps to be taken in conducting this informal analysis by students. Feel free to interpret or restructure the task in ways that best suit your own circumstances.

Clinical Task 4—INFORMAL ANALYSIS BY STUDENTS

1. Select one of the classes you are teaching and ask the students to *write out* an evaluation of that class (or perhaps the week's classes).
2. Study their written evaluations carefully. Identify some of the more common characteristics of these evaluations and note the ways in which they tend to differ from prior professional analyses.
3. Select one or two changes that have been suggested or implied by students and that seem most reasonable to you. Try to implement those changes during subsequent class meetings.

You may find the following guides helpful in planning for Task 4—they stem from past experiences with informal analyses by students.

1. The student's analysis should be written, not oral. This allows for a more lasting record. More importantly, it is highly efficient. You can collect input from thirty or more students at once and you need only 10 minutes or so of class time to do it. In the elementary school, classroom teachers might even be asked to collect the information for you. Our experience suggests that fourth- or fifth-grade children with average writing skills are old enough to provide useful written information.

2. The solicitation requesting students' input may be written on a blackboard or on the top of the students' response sheet.

3. Use a *very general* solicitation so as not to restrict the students' choice of topic (see examples below). Of course, if you want to channel their input to focus on teaching methods, or activities covered, or class organization, and so on, then put appropriate cue words in the solicitation.

4. Encourage "evaluations" or "judgments" or "opinions" from students instead of mere "descriptions" or "accounts." Unlike professionals, most students do not know how to respond if requested to "keep a record" to "tell what happened."

5. Try not to give examples of what they might say or comment on, especially to younger children; they are likely to copy it. For instance, when the teacher augments her general solicitation by saying, "For example, you might want to comment on the game we played today," 80% or 90% of the children are likely to do just that.

6. When asked to make judgments about physical education classes, students have a natural tendency to focus on subject matter activities—"I think that calisthenics stink," or "The soccer game was fun," and so on. If you want them to think beyond their reaction to specific activities, then the solicitation will have to encourage them to do so.

7. If you want to obtain reasonably specific reactions that are tied to identifiable in-class events, then suggest that the students base their reactions on what happened in the last class, or series of classes.

8. Use your own judgment to determine whether the students should sign their names to the written responses. As a general rule, anonymity will allow for freer and more honest responses.

Following are some examples of solicitations that might be used for gathering student responses:

Evaluate this physical education class (or the last three classes). Comment on anything you think is very important—such as teaching methods, activities, organization, personal experiences you've had, etc.

In your opinion, what are some of the most important changes that could be made to improve this physical education class?

Evaluate this physical education class. Try to give reasons for each of your evaluations.

What do you do with the results?

It's not easy to figure out what to do with twenty or thirty informal student analyses. After all, they do come from a variety of sources, vary considerably in quality, touch on an enormous variety of topics and issues, contradict one another, and, taken together, may not add up to anything or lead anywhere.

Perhaps the first thing to do is to read them over with the understanding that *each one represents the legitimate point of view of a very important person in that class—an individual student.* If this is all you ever do with them, it may have been worth the effort.

Try not to discredit them for their inadequacies. Sure, they are subjective, biased, self-serving, fragmentary, and so on; but then so were the informal professional analyses you completed earlier.

Once you accept these evaluations for what they are, it might be profitable to ask yourself: "In what ways do these students' perceptions of teaching and physical education tend to differ from professional perceptions?" "What kinds of things do they attend to that I hadn't thought of before?" "Are there aspects of teaching that I regard as trivial but which they seem to regard as paramount?" If you've never done this sort of thing before, serious pursuit of the answers to these questions should begin to lead you toward a broader awareness of teaching—an awareness that encompasses the perspective of the learner.

Finally, see if you can use these student evaluations to prescribe and carry out selected changes (Task 4, step 3). In doing so, it is probably wise to start out by selecting those student-suggested changes which you most strongly agree with. That is, search for the points of agreement between yourself and students, and move on them. Resolving the points of disagreement can be handled later on. If you proceed all the way to the point of implementing student-suggested changes, congratulate yourself. You can now be numbered among an elite group of exceptionally responsive teachers.

WHAT HAVE YOU DONE SO FAR?

If you have been able to complete the clinical tasks in this section, you've made a substantial start toward developing competence in the analysis of teaching.

You used a variety of approaches to analyze teaching: informal analysis of others, informal self-analysis, informal analysis by students, and a more structured analysis of intended changes. You are aware of the characteristics of these approaches and appreciate their strengths and limitations. As a consequence, you can judge their appropriateness as tools for accomplishing various educational purposes. At this time, if someone asked you to informally analyze his or her class, you could do so with ease, and with a realistic sense of what you were and were not doing.

Your awareness of your own perspective on teaching has been enhanced. You know more clearly than before those elements of teaching that you tend to focus on and value. You are more attuned to how this perspective compares with the views of others, colleagues as well as students. In fact, your own perspective may have been broadened by exposure to these other points of view.

You have used the information gleaned from informal analyses to plan and implement change. Furthermore, you have monitored the change to verify its viability and success.

Also, don't overlook the fact that you have records of the entire undertaking, incomplete though they may be, records that can improve your recollections and enhance future applications.

Finally, and by no means insignificantly, you may have improved one or more aspects of your own teaching.

FOR THE ENTHUSIAST*
Field notes

If you see value in informal analysis, but at the same time recognize a need to improve the process, try taking *field notes,* an observational and recording procedure used by researchers in the social sciences (Bickman, 1976). In essence, taking field notes is an attempt to compile a more complete record of important events so that the observer has a reasonably valid basis for analyzing what happened. Some guides for taking field notes appear below; they represent a modified version of the more exacting and time-consuming procedures normally employed by researchers.

1. Before observing a class, chat with the teacher about what she or he hopes to accomplish, the way the class will be organized and run, and anything else about the class that the teacher thinks would be important for you to know in advance.

2. Before class begins, jot down notes about the setting—e.g., number of students, grade level, facilities, etc.

3. During class, jot down notes which *describe* what happened chronologically. Try to account for what the teacher does, what the students do, and major aspects of class organization. Make sure you *describe* an event before you evalu-

---

*You'll find sections entitled For the Enthusiast at various points in this book. They are for the brave souls who have the time and inclination to pursue the analysis of teaching in depth.

ate it or indicate what should have been done. Don't get carried away and try to write down every little thing that happens. One or two pages of notes should suffice for an average 40-minute class.

4. After class, read over the notes and fill in any major gaps in the narrative. Then add important evaluative judgments that seem warranted.

You should end up with a reasonably thorough narrative description and evaluation of what happened that differs in some important ways from your initial informal analysis (Task 1). This record of events will be more complete and, hence, likely to be more meaningful and useful as a future reference. The bases on which you made your judgments should be clearer. And you will have made your observations and judgments with a better understanding of the teacher's intentions. Of course, despite these changes, recognize that the record is still quite subjective and fragmentary.

Having gone to all the trouble of taking field notes, you may want to share them with the teacher you observed—perhaps they contain some useful suggestions for improvement. Or you may have had enough of informal analysis for now. In either event, your experience in taking field notes is likely to influence the way you approach informal analysis in the future.

Critical incidents

Most analyses of teaching deal with the observation and assessment of a continuous stream of events that occur during a class. Such analyses frequently allow the most critical events to become submerged in accounts of more trivial happenings. Often it is not the stream of events but the one crucial event that makes the difference in a class. The impact of a single teacher-student interchange, for example, may be more decisive than everything else that happens to that student during a class, or even during a semester.

The Critical Incident Technique can be used to gather information about such crucial events in teaching. Developed several years ago by John Flanagan (1954), the technique has been used extensively in educational research to identify critical components of the teaching-learning process. Essentially it involves collecting relatively detailed descriptions of specific incidents and then analyzing the crucial/common elements in the descriptions.

While critical incidents can be recorded by colleagues, supervisors, or the teachers themselves, I suggest that you collect critical incidents from your students. Our studies utilizing critical incidents from physical education students (Barclay, 1968; Garis, 1964; Gibson, 1969) demonstrate that students are capable of providing remarkably informative accounts of crucial events in class. Use an approach similar to the one used in "Informal Analyses by Students" (Task 4): collect written descriptions of incidents from all students in your class, only this time use a solicitation that encourages them to provide a description of an important incident that involved them—preferably an incident that decisively affected their learning or attitude. The idea is to elicit a specific account of what happened and why it was significant. (Students as young as fifth- and sixth-graders can provide adequate accounts.) An example of the kind of solicitation that might be used is the following:

Think of the experiences you have had in this class during the past week. Describe the one experience (or incident) that helped you most in learning (name activity/skill). *Be specific;* describe what was actually said or done and by whom; and explain why it was helpful.

The wording can be changed to have students focus on "what the teacher said or did," on affective experiences, on "harmful" experiences, or some other type of incident.

Once you have collected the incidents, read them over and underline (or highlight in some other way) the most informative features of the descriptions. Search for commonalities among incidents that identify crucial aspects of your teaching or that suggest needed changes.

2

Analyzing student behavior

Educational programs are designed to facilitate student learning. Much of that learning is supposed to occur in school as a consequence of the experiences students have in classes. It stands to reason that we can find out much about the teaching/learning process by carefully studying student behavior in class. Recent studies of student behavior in physical education classes have produced some surprising results. For example, Costello (1977, 1978) studied the behavior of 192 students in twenty different elementary classes and found that they spent only 28.7% of their time actively engaged in movement activities, while the bulk of their time was spent "waiting" (35.4%) or "receiving information" from the teacher (25.4%). These results and similar findings in other studies have raised questions about whether physical education class time is being used efficiently.

How about the students in your classes—how do they spend their time? What sort of opportunities do they have for practice? Play? Instruction? Exercise? Don't be too quick to answer. Your subjective impressions of student behavior may not be consistent with objective reality. This chapter is designed to equip you with techniques for carefully studying student behavior, and to provide you with a clear and objective picture of student behavior in your classes.

DESCRIPTIVE ANALYSIS*

An approach called "descriptive analysis" will be employed to record student behavior. It differs in a number of important ways from the informal analysis you have just experienced. The approach is planned. In advance you will know rather precisely what to look for during the observation, and what to do when you see it. You will "describe" student behavior (rather than evaluate it) by classifying behaviors into predefined categories—a process we call "coding." The record that

---

*In recent years "descriptive analysis" has been used extensively in research on teaching. Our own Data Bank studies at Teachers College, Columbia University, have developed and used several "descriptive systems" to analyze events in physical education classes. The descriptive-analytic approaches in this chapter and elsewhere in this text are based, in part, on one or more of our research projects. Of course, the approaches suggested here have been drastically simplified to facilitate their use in teacher education settings.

emerges will be comparatively objective and reliable.* That is, two people using this approach to code the same students in the same class should come up with similar records; and if you recoded the same students' behavior during the same class (from a videotaped recording), both records would be similar. Thus the information recorded is often referred to as *data* because it so closely resembles a factual description of what occurred rather than the subjective impressions and opinions of the observer.

Three introductory techniques for coding student behavior are covered in this chapter. They are a small sample of the vast array of coding procedures available and focus on only a few of the countless aspects of student behavior that might be examined. To familiarize yourself with each technique, start by coding students in someone else's class. If you are fortunate enough to have a videotape available, have someone tape your own class and then you code the tape. It is hoped that the data collected will provide a meaningful basis for making decisions about how to conduct subsequent classes. If the need for change is indicated, you should plan the changes, reteach the class, and recode student behavior to determine whether the change produced the desired result.

HOW ARE THEY SPENDING THEIR TIME?

Students often spend only two or three periods a week in gym—perhaps 60 to 100 minutes of actual contact time. That is not a lot of time, so it needs to be spent judiciously if we hope to accomplish our objectives.

One way to obtain a meaningful account of students' behavior is to record the time they spend in different types of activity, and particularly to distinguish between those types of activities that are likely to contribute to educational outcomes and those that are not. Clinical Task 5 suggests that you code 3-minute samples of the behavior of one student at a time during a class. A time-sampling technique is recommended—code for 3 minutes, relax for 3 minutes—to make it easier on you. Coding only one student at a time is mandatory if you hope to achieve an accurate record. It is virtually impossible to code two students at once with any degree of accuracy. Select a student whose behavior you are interested in for one reason or another—perhaps an "average" student whose behavior might reflect what the average students are doing, or perhaps a special individual whose behavior you would like to know more about.

To complete this Clinical Task you will have to prepare and use a *coding form*. A sample form appears on p. 25. This one has already been used to code the

---

*High levels of objectivity and reliability are obtained in research studies using descriptive analysis. We normally achieve 85% to 99% agreement between trained coders using carefully developed descriptive systems. Of course, lower levels of agreement can be expected when using the approaches suggested here since the categories and coding procedures are less precisely defined and your training as an observer is minimal.

behavior of a student in an elementary school gymnastics class. Study the form for a moment to better understand the kind of record that emerges from this type of analysis.

To code behavior accurately and consistently, definitions of categories of behavior are needed. The Category Definitions on p. 24 delineate the boundaries of the six broad categories you will use in completing Clinical Task 5. They are a simplified and restructured version of the categories developed by Laubach (1975). The major thrust of this particular set of categories is to distinguish between behaviors that normally contribute to the achievement of educational outcomes (performs motor activity, receives information) and those that do not (waits, relocates, and other). Study these definitions before attempting to code a student.

The Coding Procedures, p. 24, tell you how to carry out the coding. Notice that you are to code behavior for each 5-second interval. We've settled on 5-second intervals because shorter intervals make coding too laborious and require training, and longer intervals encompass too many different kinds of events to be useful. Furthermore, we use interval recordings rather than exact duration timing (i.e., timing each behavior to the second) because accurate duration timing is not possible unless you code from videotapes which can be stopped and replayed.

You will undoubtedly encounter some difficulty in making coding decisions. After all, real-world events occur in a continuous stream, not in 5-second intervals; many events don't fall neatly into a category but in some gray area between categories; and even 5-second intervals often contain more than one type of behavior. To help resolve some of these difficulties, follow the "special ground rules" on p. 24.

At this point, please don't be scared off by what may appear to be an imposing coding task. It's really quite easy once you get into it. It takes teachers only about one-half hour to learn to use this approach with reasonable proficiency.

Clinical Task 5—CODING STUDENT TIME IN ACTIVITIES

1. Identify a target student whose behavior you will code during the class.
2. Use the category definitions, coding procedures, ground rules, and record form (p. 24) to code the students' behavior during alternate 3-minute segments of the class.
3. Compute the total time and percentage of time spent in each category of activity.
4. Study the record. Make notes under Summary Comments and Evaluation about any features of the record which strike you as important—particularly those features which have a bearing on how well the student spent his or her time.
5. Have someone else code a target student in one of the classes you teach.

DEFINITIONS, PROCEDURES, AND GROUND RULES FOR CODING STUDENT TIME IN ACTIVITIES

Category definitions

1. *Performs motor activity:* Actively engages in motor task normally considered to be the subject matter of physical education, including: playing game or sport, practicing skill, performing exercise or calisthenics, and exploring solutions to movement problems.
2. *Receives information:* Listens to teacher or other student; attends to demonstration, audiovisual aid, or written material.
3. *Gives information or assists:* Talks to other students or teacher (includes asking questions); demonstrates, manually assists, or spots for others.
4. *Waits:* Engages in "holding" behavior—e.g., waiting his turn, waiting for game to begin, etc. Is not performing motor activity or giving or receiving information.
5. *Relocates:* Moves from one place to another, such as walking from one activity area to another, or walking to get on line. Is not giving or receiving information.
6. *Other:* Engages in activity other than those mentioned above, such as obtaining equipment, getting drink of water, tying shoes, etc.

Coding procedures

1. Select a target student.
2. Select an appropriate starting point. Code the student's behavior for 3 minutes; then rest for 3 minutes; then code for 3 minutes; and so on.
3. Code behavior at the end of every 5-second interval by placing a check in the category that *best describes* the type of behavior the student engaged in during that interval.
4. At the end of each 3-minute interval use the "notations" column to record any comments that will help you to recollect specific events in the coding segment.
5. At the conclusion of the period, total the checks in each column and calculate the percentage of time spent in each type of activity. Make appropriate entries under Summary Comments and Evaluation.

Special ground rules

1. If two or more types of behavior occur during an interval, code the type of behavior that consumed the greater portion of the interval. For example, if the student "waited" for 2 seconds and practiced for 3 seconds, code as "performed motor activity."
2. If two types of behavior occur *simultaneously* for the major portion of an interval (which sometimes happens when students receive information while they are performing a motor activity), code both behaviors.
3. Consider the student to be performing a motor activity when she or he is executing a movement, or in a "ready position," or completing a follow through; or if a game is being played, consider the student to be performing when "time is in" for her or him.

SAMPLE CODING FORM AND RECORD

TIME SAMPLING OF A SINGLE STUDENT'S BEHAVIOR

RECORD A CHECK (✓) FOR EACH
5 SECONDS OF STUDENT ACTIVITY.

STUDENT'S NAME: _Alice Smith_

CLASS: _Elementary Gymnastics_

SEGMENT (3-min.)	PERFORMS MOTOR ACTIVITY	RECEIVES INFOR-MATION	GIVES INFORMA-TION OR ASSISTS	WAITS	RELOCATES	OTHER	NOTATIONS
I 9:00–9:03	✓✓✓ ③	✓✓✓✓ ✓✓✓✓ ✓✓✓ ⑳		✓✓✓✓✓ ✓✓✓✓ ⑩	✓✓ ②	✓ ①	Waited for teacher to begin Rec. info on class organization
II 9:06–9:09	✓✓✓✓ ✓✓✓ ⑧	✓✓✓✓✓ ✓✓✓✓✓ ✓✓✓✓✓ ✓✓✓✓✓ ✓✓ ㉒		✓✓ ②	✓✓✓ ③	✓ ①	End instruction / began tumbling and head stand
III 9:12–9:15	✓✓✓✓✓ ✓✓✓✓ ✓✓✓✓ ✓✓ ⑰	✓✓✓✓✓ ⑤	✓✓✓✓✓ ⑤	✓✓ ②	✓ ①	✓✓✓✓✓ ✓ ⑥	Cont'd tumbling "Other" = replaced mats
IV 9:18–9:21	✓✓✓✓✓ ✓✓✓✓ ✓✓✓✓✓ ✓✓ ㉒	✓✓✓ ③	✓✓✓ ③	✓✓✓✓✓ ⑤		✓✓✓ ③	Performed on ropes
V 9:24–9:27	✓✓✓ ③	✓✓✓✓✓ ✓✓✓✓✓ ✓✓✓✓✓ ✓✓✓✓✓ ✓✓✓✓✓ ㉕		✓✓✓ ③	✓✓✓ ③	✓✓ ②	Rec'd instruction on bars
VI 9:30–9:33	✓✓✓ ③	✓✓✓✓✓ ✓✓ ✓✓✓ ⑩		✓✓✓✓ ✓✓✓✓✓ ✓✓✓✓✓ ✓✓✓✓✓ ✓ ㉑		✓✓ ②	Waits turn on bars and performs
TOTALS	f = 56 % = 56/216 = 26%	f = 85 % = 85/216 = 39%	f = 8 % = 8/216 = 3%	f = 43 % = 43/216 = 19%	f = 9 % = 9/216 = 4%	f = 15 % = 15/216 = 7%	

SUMMARY COMMENTS AND EVALUATION (made by teacher of class)

Too much time spent waiting for teacher and getting organized.
Good activity levels on mats and ropes — too much waiting around on bars.
Overall, a greater proportion of time should be spent in performing activities.

HOW MUCH PRACTICE ARE THEY GETTING?

If there is one thing most physical educators have in common, it's a concern for improving the students' proficiency in motor skills or tasks. Since improved proficiency comes with practice, most teachers are reasonably committed to providing adequate amounts* of in-class practice for their students.

Our informal analyses of classes often yield misleading impressions as to how much and what kinds of practice students are getting. We scan a gymnastics class with eight different practice stations and gain the impression of profuse and varied activity—when in fact most students spend 90% of their time waiting their turn. We watch a soccer game and perceive 15 or 20 minutes of continuous motor activity—and yet fail to notice that several players never come in contact with the ball.

One very simple way to obtain an objective account of how much practice students get is to observe a student and *count* the number of practice trials he or she experiences during a selected period of time. This is precisely what Clinical Task 6 asks you to do.

The analytic technique suggested here is similar to the one used in Task 5. You follow one student at a time and describe what he or she is doing by coding behavior into preselected categories. This time, however, you will have to generate your own categories based on the skills/tasks that students in the target class will have an opportunity to perform. Furthermore, instead of coding at 5-second intervals, you code only when the *event* occurs, in this case a practice trial. Finally, you needn't code the student for the entire period but instead might choose a logical time segment for observation—perhaps a practice session, or a game, or free play time.

All in all, this method of analysis is very easy to use, and the records it yields can be fascinating. You'll obtain a much more specific account of the students' motor activity than you did in Clinical Task 5 (although the account won't be continuous). Furthermore, you will have a reasonably objective record of not only the amount of practice trials, but the distribution of practice across the different tasks available.

By the way, because I use the term "practice," don't think this analytic technique is applicable only to formal sports skills practice sessions. It can be used to analyze student performance in games of low organization, lead-up games, movement education lessons, and formal competitive games. Simply identify the fundamental movement tasks or skills involved in the game or lesson, define them, and then code.

---

*Obviously the *quality* of practice is at least as important as the amount. Qualitative features of practice are dealt with in subsequent Clinical Tasks.

You will have to give some thought to defining what constitutes a legitimate practice trial of a given skill or task. Whatever rules you use to help make this determination, I suggest you jot them down so they can be applied consistently from observation to observation. As a general rule it's wise to be liberal in your definition of a trial—let even the most meager attempts count. Later on, when we come to qualitative analysis of student performance, you will have a chance to distinguish the more or less successful trials.

Clinical Task 6—CODING STUDENT PRACTICE TRIALS

1. Identify a target student whose behavior you will code during the class.
2. Identify the key skills or motor tasks the student will have an opportunity to perform during the class. Compose a record form for recording trials on each skill or task (see Sample Records, p. 28).
3. Code the student's behavior during a class, or a segment of a class.
4. Study the record. Make notes under Summary Comments and Evaluation about any features of the record that strike you as important. In particular give consideration to the adequacy of the amount and distribution of trials.
5. Have someone else code the practice trials of a student in one of the classes you teach.

SAMPLE CODING FORMS AND RECORDS

STUDENT TRIALS ON KEY SKILLS/TASKS

SOCCER GAMES

	STUDENT #1 FIRST PERIOD	STUDENT #2 SECOND PERIOD
PASS	√	
TRAP	√√√	
HEAD	√√	
CLEAR	√√√√√√	√√
TACKLE	√√√√	
DRIBBLE	√√√	
SHOT		
THROW IN	√√√	√
CORNER DEFENSE FREE PENALTY } KICK	√√	
SAVE		

GYMNASTICS

	STUDENT #1 FOURTH PERIOD	STUDENT #2 SIXTH PERIOD
FORWARD ROLL	√√√√√√√	√
BACKWARD ROLL	√	√
STRADDLE ROLL	√	√
CARTWHEEL		√√√
ROUND OFF		√√√√√
HEADSTAND	√	
MULE KICK		
HANDSTAND		√√
LIMBER		√
BACK WALK-OVER		√√√√√√√
FRONT WALK-OVER		√√
DIVE ROLL		
FRONT HAND SPRING		

SUMMARY COMMENTS AND EVALUATION

These were fourth grade classes. Games lasted 20 minutes.
Student #1 was among better players, got adequate practice.
Student #2 - a weak player; this was a waste of time for her.

Sixth grade classes, during 15 minutes of free mat time at end of period.
Student #1 stuck to the one thing he could do well - could have made many more attempts.
Student #2 - used time efficiently - worked on two skills that needed improvement.

EXPANDING THE STUDENT SAMPLE BY SPOT-CHECKING

Previous techniques for coding student behavior (Clinical Tasks 5 and 6) yield a record of the actions of one student or a few students in a class; these records may or may not be a reliable index of the behavior of selected groups of students or of the entire class. When it is important for you to find out what most or all of the students are doing, alternate coding techniques are required. For example, perhaps your class will be divided into groups which practice separately at different stations, and you want a record of how things are going at each station. Or perhaps a particular class will progress through several instructional stages— e.g., from large group lecture, to individualized practice, to small group critiques, to summary and review—and you want to know what all students are doing in each stage.

A technique called spot-checking* is useful for these purposes. It involves quickly scanning the behavior of several or all students during a short interval (10 to 20 seconds) and classifying the behavior of each student into one of two (or possibly one of three) categories. The record of behavior for the interval is a count of students whose behaviors fall in one category or the other.

Sample spot-check records appear on pp. 30-31. The record on p. 30 shows the number of students performing and not performing motor activities during an elementary school basketball class. Ten spot-checks were made, once every 3 minutes—each spot-check took 5 to 10 seconds to complete. The record on p. 31 is that of a high school gymnastics class. Spot-checks were taken every 2 minutes to determine the on-task/off-task behavior of students. Here a separate record was compiled for each of the four teaching stations in the class by rotating the spot-checks among the stations.

I hope these two illustrations suggest the variety of ways the spot-checking technique can be applied. You might spot-check the behavior of the whole class at fixed intervals, spot-check a selected group of students throughout the class, or check student behavior at a particular station throughout the class; or check behavior at several stations on a rotating basis, concentrate the spot-checks within one segment of the class, and so on. The type of spot-check selected should depend on the structure of the particular class and on what you want to find out about it.

Since spot-checks involve only momentary perceptions of each individual student, the classification of student behavior has to be kept very simple—hence the recommendation that only two or at most three categories be used. This allows

---

*Many different names have been applied to this generic technique, or to particular variations of the technique. The term Placheck, developed by Hall (1970) and applied to physical education settings by Siedentop (1976), is one popular variation.

SAMPLE SPOT-CHECK RECORD

CLASS I — Fifth grade class: plays "basketball relay" (24 students)

TIME	ACTIVELY PERFORMS MOTOR ACTIVITY*	INACTIVE** (NOT PERFORMING MOTOR ACTIVITY)	NOTES
9:05	0	24	students listening to instructions
9:08	24	0	students doing mass calisthenics
9:11	18	6	jogging, some have finished
9:14	3	21	relay, 3 lines
9:17	3	21	relay, 3 lines
9:20	0	24	instructions between relays
9:23	3	21	resume relay
9:30	3	21	relay
9:33	0	24	review scores
9:36	0	24	dismissal
Total	54	186	

Percent active $54/240 = 22.5\%$

SUMMARY COMMENTS AND EVALUATION

Overall the basketball relay did not provide sufficient activity and practice for the students given the total amount of class time it consumed.

* Actively performs motor activity: practices skills, plays game, explores movement, performs exercise, performs other substantive movement.

** Inactive (not performing motor activity): waits, listens, relocates, and other actions not considered to be performing motor activity.

SAMPLE SPOT-CHECK RECORD

CLASS II — High School Gymnastics class (32 students)

STATION	TIME	ON-TASK ACTIVE*	ON-TASK INACTIVE**	OFF-TASK***	NOTES
I Beam	10:00	1	6	1	most watching
	10:08	1	5	2	2 wandered off
	10:16	2	4	2	2 conversation, 1 spotter
	10:24	0		8	no activity, all socializing
II Unevens	10:02	2	6	0	one or two spotters — teacher giving instruction
	10:10	3	4	1	one person assisting
	10:18	2	2	4	4 socializing
	10:26	1	3	3	3 socializing
III Vaulting	10:04	3	4	1	one performer, two spotters
	10:12	3	5	0	
	10:20	3	3	2	} 2-3 walked to
	10:28	3	2	3	} other station
IV Mats	10:06	6	2	0	all 6 performing
	10:14	7	1	0	2 assisting, 5 performing
	10:22	5	1	2	
	10:30	4	0	4	4 fooling around

SUMMARY COMMENTS AND EVALUATION

Most active performance occurs on mats.
Spotting is inadequate on beam, good on vaulting.
Off-task activity increases toward end of period.

---

* On-task active = performs, spots, assists.
** On-task inactive = watches performance, listens.
*** Off-task = socializes, wanders off, apparent daydreaming, etc.

the observer to quickly scan individuals within a group and keep track (mentally) of the number who are or are not doing something, and then record those numbers. It is not possible to do this using four or more categories—multiple categories force you to record behavior on a student-by-student basis and to observe each student for longer intervals (as in Clinical Task 5).

In completing Clinical Task 7, the choice of categories is up to you. The two sets of categories used in the two sample records (pp. 30-31)—active/inactive and on-task/off-task—are commonly used in spot-checking. They provide a gross indication of whether students are involved in productive activity (active) or not, and whether they are doing what they are supposed to (on-task) or not. Other dichotomous sets of categories that might prove useful are: safe/unsafe, attentive/ inattentive, cooperative/disruptive, and interacting with others/isolated. Whatever categories you choose, they should reflect a significant aspect of the particular class being observed. Also, you should define each category in advance by listing the activities that fall under it.

In performing the spot-check itself, try the following:
1. Scan from left to right across the gym.
2. Classify the behavior of each individual student at the moment your eyes come in contact with him or her.
3. Keep count (mentally) of the less frequently occurring behavior category (e.g., in an active class keep count of the inactives; in a well-behaved class keep count of the misbehaviors; etc.).
4. Record the total for the less frequently occurring behavior; then subtract it from the total number of students in the class (or group) to obtain the total for the more frequent behavior.
5. Take notes at the end of each spot-check to help you recall important aspects of what was taking place.

Clinical Task 7—SPOT-CHECKING STUDENT BEHAVIOR

1. Given your understanding of the potential and limitations of spot-checking, choose a class about which spot-checks will yield useful information.
2. Use active/inactive or on-task/off-task categories as defined in Sample Records, pp. 30-31; or develop and define a set of categories of your own.
3. Decide on the behavior to be sampled—i.e., whole class/group, by station, number of checks, etc.
4. Develop a coding form, and code using the procedures suggested above.
5. Study the record. Make summary comments and evaluations of any features of the record that strike you as important.
6. Have someone use spot-checking to code the behavior of students in a class you teach.

CHARACTERISTICS OF STUDENT CODINGS

Once you have completed Clinical Tasks 5, 6, and 7, take some time to examine the characteristics of the analytic approaches used.

In each instance your observation and analysis had a preplanned focus. You defined behavioral categories and followed certain rules in collecting data and in sampling student behavior. You have accounted for the ways in which selected students distributed their time among certain types of activities (Task 5), and the number and kinds of practice trials engaged in by other students (Task 6). You spot-checked the behavior of large numbers of students according to certain gross behavioral classifications (Task 7). The resulting records should be reasonably objective and reliable, although this will depend to some extent on the care with which the coding procedures were followed.

I'm sure by this time you are keenly aware of the *descriptive* nature of the emergent records; that is, they tell much about *what* the students were doing and very little about *how well* they were doing it.* If you reacted as most professionals do when first confronted with descriptive coding tasks, there were probably many occasions when you desperately wanted to rate the quality of student performances and were somewhat frustrated by the constraints of descriptive coding. The emphasis here has been on "getting the facts" first (i.e., descriptive record), and then using those data to make evaluations.

Recognize some of the limitations of the approaches used. First, in each approach you've obtained a limited sample of student behavior in a given class. In two instances (Tasks 5 and 6) you know what only one student is doing at selected times during the class; you don't know what the student is doing at other times, nor do you know what all the rest of the students are doing. In the third instance (Task 7) you know what all students or groups of students are doing at selected moments, but not what they are doing at other times. The extent to which these time samples are a legitimate representation of the behavior of the entire class is always questionable. Furthermore, you only "know" what the students were doing in terms of the limited set of categories used for classifying behavior. All other aspects of behavior go unrecorded and perhaps unnoticed, except for some items that appear as notations accompanying the record. Indeed, you don't know how well the students performed, whether they interacted with or responded to the teacher, whether they learned anything, and so on. As with the informal analytic approaches covered earlier, you have succeeded in capturing only a small part of what happened in the classes.

At this point I hope you see these techniques for what they are—a limited set

---

*The distinction between describing and rating or evaluating is not always clear-cut. In fact, in Task 7 if you classified behavior as cooperative/disruptive or safe/unsafe, you may have been doing more "rating" than describing.

of tools that can be used to gather certain types of information about student behavior in class, information that can be used for some purposes in some situations but not in others. Furthermore, I hope you understand that these are flexible tools that can be altered and combined in various ways to better suit the purposes of the user (see For the Enthusiast, p. 35).

MAKING CHANGES

One or more of the completed records of student behavior or the Summary Comments and Evaluation at the end of each record are likely to identify certain problems or suggest needed improvements in the observed classes. If so, it makes sense to try to change the classes (i.e., the teaching strategy, organization, subject matter, etc.) in such a way as to alleviate the problem or make the improvement (see Clinical Task 8). Obviously the problems you identify and the changes you implement will depend on the particular characteristics of the record used, on the target teaching situation, and on your own values and preferences. Some problems and possible solutions commonly identified by other teachers using these coding techniques are listed here. They may or may not be relevant to your situation.

Commonly identified problems	Possible solutions (changes)
1. Students spend too much time at beginning of period getting organized.	1. Introduce efficient organizing procedures and routines.
2. Practice setting yields too few practice trials per student.	2. Increase number of practice stations; use more equipment.
3. Lead-up game (e.g., sideline soccer, call basketball, etc.) yields too few practice trials per student.	3. Change rules of game to increase numbers of active participants; throw out game and use a different one.
4. Competitive game (e.g., volleyball, soccer, basketball, etc.) results in minimal number of skill trials for less skilled students.	4. Reduce number of players on team; change rules; group students more homogeneously; increase practice time in proportion to game time.
5. Students spend inordinately large proportion of time listening to teacher talk.	5. Stop talking so much.
6. In free practice or exploration setting student performs one task repeatedly.	6. Give instructions or challenges that increase variety in tasks chosen; have student keep record of tasks performed.
7. Off-task or disruptive student behavior increases toward end of period or during long waiting periods.	7. Clarify rules for behavior; introduce new or more challenging activities as period progresses; reduce waiting periods.
8. Dangerous misbehavior occurs at a particular practice location.	8. Clarify rules for safe behavior; stand close to location and monitor student behavior.

Clinical Task 8—USING CODINGS OF STUDENT BEHAVIOR AS A BASIS FOR CHANGING TEACHING

Using the records of student behavior in the classes you taught:
1. Review the records from Tasks 5, 6, and 7 and ask yourself:
    a. What changes in class structure, teaching behavior, etc., would yield improvement in one or more aspects of the student behavior recorded? (Compose list.)
    b. Which of these changes are immediately feasible?
    c. Which *one* or *two* of the feasible changes are most important?
2. Write out the changes identified in *c* and indicate the way in which the change should improve the record of student behavior.

3. Reteach the class or the lesson and have someone recode student behavior using one or an appropriate combination of the coding procedures from Tasks 5, 6, and 7.

4. Analyze the extent to which the change produced an improvement in the record of student behavior.

If it didn't work, try again. Change something else this time.

FOR THE ENTHUSIAST

If you find these techniques for coding student behavior to be interesting and valuable, by all means continue to use them, and feel free to vary them in ways that are best suited to your purposes. Some variations in approach that you might want to try out are listed below.

Restructuring categories

Starting with the student activity categories (Task 5, p. 24), add, delete, or refine categories to include types of student activities that you are particularly interested in monitoring. For example, you might want to divide "receives information" into "receives instructional information" and "receives other information"; or add a category for spotting. Have a colleague check over the revisions to make certain they are understandable and usable. Then use the revised categories to code student behavior.

Developing your own system

If you feel particularly adventurous, develop a category system of your own to code student behavior. This is the best way to make sure that you get at aspects of student behavior that you believe are critical. It's also much more fun than using someone else's system. If you do so, keep the set of categories simple—don't try to use more than six or eight categories at a time. Also, make sure the categories are mutually exclusive so that an observed behavior doesn't fit into more than one category. *The Classroom Observer* by Boehm and Weinberg (1977) provides some excellent guidance for those interested in developing their own system.

Combine techniques

To obtain a more complete picture of a given class, combine spot-checking and coding practice trials or spot-checking and coding time in activities.

Comparative analyses

Choose two or more classes that are organized and taught in different ways. Code student behavior in each class, compare the results, and make decisions about the efficacy of the different approaches to teaching.

Determine the objectivity of your coding

Using any one of the coding procedures (Task 5, 6, or 7) code a student(s) behavior and have a colleague simultaneously code the same behavior—but work independently, don't consult with each other during the coding. Afterward, compare your codings and calculate the percent agreement between coders as follows:

$$\text{Percent agreement} = \frac{\text{Agreements}}{\text{Total codings}}$$

where

Agreements   = number of checks made by coder 1 for which coder 2 makes a similar check in the same category during the same time period
Total codings = total number checks recorded by coder 1

If your level of agreement is low (perhaps below 80%), identify the reasons for disagreements, correct them by clarifying rules and definitions, and then repeat the process.

3

Analyzing teacher behavior

Teachers' impressions of what they do in class are often quite different from what they actually do. When teachers are presented for the first time with an objective record of the types of behaviors they exhibited in a class, they are almost invariably surprised. Being put in touch with the objective realities of one's own behavior in class can be instructive and useful. In fact, several studies indicate that providing teachers with objective feedback about their in-class performance has a profound impact on their subsequent behavior (Peck and Tucker, 1973). For concerned teachers, such feedback can be the first step in the lengthy process of bringing their overt behavior into alignment with their intentions and commitments. This chapter contains clinical experiences designed to enhance your awareness of what you do in class.

Teacher behavior in class is not easily deciphered or described. Teachers engage in an enormous variety of tasks. They shift from one type of activity to another with astounding rapidity. (One study of physical education teachers [Barrette, 1977] indicates that, on the average, a major behavioral shift occurs every 4.5 seconds.) Their behaviors are linked to one another within an intricate network of past, present, and future events. Often the intent as well as the effects of the behavior are inscrutable. And, as you now well appreciate from your experiences with informal analysis, observed behaviors are subject to various interpretations, depending on the perspective of the viewer. Given these inherent complexities, the task of describing and/or evaluating teacher behavior is a very complicated business.

The clinical tasks in this chapter, and other tasks in subsequent chapters, focus primarily on the analyses of your teaching behavior, although you will also analyze the behaviors of others. Each task or set of tasks focuses on a different aspect of teacher behavior. In effect we shall attempt to better understand your behavior by systematically picking it apart and studying one piece at a time, recognizing as we proceed that we are in fact dealing with one piece of a much larger puzzle. As the pieces accrue, we hope some features of the puzzle will take shape, although it would be naive to expect that we will ever complete the picture.

BASIC DIMENSIONS OF TEACHER BEHAVIOR

A reasonable starting point for the study of teacher behavior is to focus on certain basic dimensions of interactive behavior. (Interactive behavior involves conveying or receiving messages to/from others via talking, listening, demonstrating, observing, etc.) Teachers spend most of their in-class time interacting with students. A recent study (Anderson and Barrette, 1978) shows that physical education teachers spend about 95% of their class time interacting with students. When a teacher interacts she or he does so in a particular way, with some person or group, about something, in order to accomplish some purpose. Said another way, the teacher's behavior has a *function* (purpose), *mode* (way of interacting), *direction* (persons with whom the teacher interacts), and *substance* (topic or subject of the interaction).

Each segment of interactive teacher behavior can be classified and described according to these dimensions: function, mode, direction, and substance. When a teacher says, "Johnny, dribble the ball lower," this event can be described as: giving instruction or corrective feedback (function), by talking (mode), to one student (direction), about dribbling (substance). The function, mode, direction, and substance of teacher behavior will serve as the focus for Clinical Tasks 9, 10, and 11. Our strategy will be to code and analyze one or two dimensions at a time—trying to do them all at once is too demanding unless videotape is used.

The coding techniques used will resemble those employed previously in describing student behavior. You will start by coding the behavior of another teacher, then have someone else code your behavior. The intent will be to amass a descriptive record that is reasonably objective and reliable, then use that record as a basis for evaluation and change.

WHAT FUNCTION IS THE TEACHER CARRYING OUT?

Teaching is normally conceived of as a purposeful activity. When teachers teach, when teachers talk about what they do, when authors write about teaching, when lessons are planned, and when teaching is evaluated, there is almost always the implicit or explicit assumption that discrete acts have a purpose. Physical education is no exception. Its literature, research concepts, and terminology are dominated by references to purpose or function. It seems reasonable, therefore, to start this examination of teacher behavior by accounting for the functions carried out by that behavior.

One way* to describe teacher functions is to employ commonly used professional terminology and concepts to classify behavior. Physical educators have a

---

*Needless to say, there is an enormous variety of ways to describe the purpose or function of teacher behavior. Ample evidence of this is found in the hundreds of existing analytic systems (Dunkin and Biddle, 1974; Simon and Boyer, 1970), each of which conceptualizes function in different ways. The challenge facing us is to select a way that best suits our purpose at this time.

common language that they use to describe many of the distinctive teaching tasks they perform. A teacher performing a skill in order to show students how it should be done is "demonstrating"; a teacher standing next to a student performer to protect the student from injury is "spotting"; and so on. The virtue of describing teacher function in terms of these common professional classifications is that they yield a description that can be easily interpreted and used by the professionals.

I developed a system for coding teacher behavior in physical education according to common professional functions (Anderson, 1974). Barrette (1977) used the system to code the videotaped behavior of forty physical education teachers. As a group, these teachers spent 36.9% of their time giving instruction to students, 21.1% silently monitoring student performance of motor activity, 15.7% performing various class and behavior management functions, 7.5% officiating, and 18.8% in carrying out a variety of other functions. Teacher-to-teacher variations were sizable; for example, some teachers spent as little as 2% of their time giving instruction, while others devoted more than 80% to instruction (Barrette, 1977). What about your own behavior? How do you apportion your time in class? Are you using that time wisely?

In Clinical Task 9 your behavior will be coded according to professional function. The function categories to be used are a consolidation and simplification of the categories in my original system. Notice that the categories are designed to reflect common features of physical education classes, especially with respect to the role of motor activities as a focal point for interaction. The intent is to provide you with an easy-to-use set of categories that will yield a professionally meaningful description of your behavior.

Clinical Task 9—CODING TEACHER BEHAVIOR ACCORDING TO PROFESSIONAL FUNCTION

1. Study the category definitions, coding procedures, ground rules, examples of coding, and coding form (pp. 40-41). Practice coding on a few occasions until you can do so accurately and efficiently.
2. Select a class taught by another teacher and code the teacher's behavior continuously for as much of the period as possible. If the procedure gets burdensome, take a rest, and then begin again; keep a record of the rest periods on your coding form.
3. Compute the total frequency and percentage of time spent performing each function.
4. Show the record to the teacher whose behavior was coded and, together with that teacher, make appropriate entries under Summary Comments and Evaluation.
5. Have someone code your behavior as you teach a class, then complete steps 3 and 4. Or, if you have a videotape of your own teaching performance, code it yourself.

DEFINITIONS, PROCEDURES, AND GROUND RULES FOR CODING TEACHER FUNCTION

Category definitions

(I)   *Instructing:* Providing information about the subject matter of physical education (such as movement concepts, motor skill performance, game rules, and strategies), with the intent that students learn it. The information may be provided directly by the teacher talking or demonstrating; or indirectly by soliciting information from students, having a student demonstrate, using audiovisual aids, etc. Includes preparatory instruction as well as providing students with feedback about their performance.

(M) *Monitoring motor activities:* Silently attending to student(s) who are performing motor activities* (not actively guiding or instructing).

(F)   *Officiating/regulating motor activities:* Performing the recognized and established duties of an official in a game or sport. Also includes performing the duties of an official (i.e., regulating the starting and stopping of activities, enforcing rules, keeping time, keeping score) in a game or activity for which there are no established rules.

(C)   *Class management: Organizing* students for activity by grouping, assigning location or position. Performing *administrative* tasks such as taking attendance, making announcements, setting schedules, etc. Providing or adjusting *equipment,* or readying the environment.

(B)   *Behavior management:* Interacting with students about compliance with classroom norms and rules for social-personal conduct. Includes disciplining, praising proper behavior, explaining rules, etc., but *not* related to subject matter.

(X)   *Other:* Includes *participating* in motor activities (not demonstrating); *spotting* interacting with students about matters other than those mentioned in the preceding categories; *noninteractive* intervals when the teacher is not communicating with or observing students.

Note to the coder: Six separate coding categories have been designated—I, M, F, C, B, X. If you find these easy to use and would like to code behavior more specifically, add separate categories for participating (P), spotting (S), other interacting (XI), noninteractive (X).

---

*Motor activities are those goal-directed movement activities normally considered to be part of the subject matter of physical education, such as games, sports, exercises, motor skills practice, exploratory movements, and fundamental movements.

Coding procedures

1. Focus on the teacher's behavior, and ask yourself "What function is he or she performing?"
2. Code the teacher's behavior at the end of *approximately** every 5-second interval by writing down the code letter of the category that best describes the function of the teacher's behavior during the interval. (See Sample Coding Form, p. 43.)
3. Use any blank sheet of lined paper for coding. Write codes sequentially in a vertical column, one code per line. Use an arrow to indicate the continuation of a behavior for several intervals. When you reach the bottom of the page, start a new column. (See Sample Coding Form.)
4. Make any notations you wish next to the codings to help you to recollect events that appear to be significant.
5. At the conclusion of the period, total the codings in each category and calculate the approximate percentage of time spent in each category using:

$$\frac{\text{no. of codings for category}}{\text{no. of lines (intervals) on coding form}}$$

Make appropriate entries under Summary Comments and Evaluation.

Special ground rules

1. When two or more functions are carried out during the same interval, record the appropriate multiple codes on the same line. (NOTE: these multiple codes will tend to inflate the total percentages derived for certain categories.)
2. When the teacher tells/asks the student(s) to carry out one of the listed functions, use the function category which best describes the function the students are carrying out.
3. When the teacher is engaged in a verbal interchange with a student(s), use the function category which best describes the purpose of the entire interchange.
4. Whenever you are uncertain about the function being carried out by the teacher, code it as "other."

---

*The coding need not be done precisely at each 5-second mark. You may use natural breaks in behavior as the basis for delineating an interval. For example, if the teacher gives instruction for 6 or 7 seconds and then monitors activity for 3 or 4 seconds, simply code it as I followed by M.

EXAMPLES OF CODING TEACHER FUNCTION

Events	Code
Teacher starts period by saying, "Everyone please sit on the white circle."	C (class management)
Teacher watches as students go to circle.	C
Teacher calls names for attendance.	C
Student asks teacher about schedule for the following week, teacher responds.	C
Teacher says, "Let's start our stretching exercises, keep in time with me—one-two-three."	F (officiating/regulatory)
Teacher stops counting and watches students do remainder of exercises.	M (monitoring motor activity)
Teacher says, "Today we'll continue our work on jump shooting; remember, now, the idea is to control the ball with the wrist and fingertips . . ."	I (instruction)
Teacher says, "All members of the red team get a ball and practice shooting at the far end of the gym . . ."	C
Teacher watches students get ball and move to end of the gym.	C
Teacher watches as students begin to practice shooting.	M
Teacher watches Johnny shoot the ball and says, "No, Johnny, you're not using your wrist . . ."	I
Teacher demonstrates correct shooting form for Johnny.	I
Jimmy asks the teacher if he can go to the bathroom, teacher says yes.	C
Teacher gazes out the window, then stops to tie his shoe.	X (other noninteractive)
Teacher notices Mike pushing Mary and says, "Mike, cut that out. You know that's not allowed in gym."	B (behavior management)
Teacher says to Peggy, "I understand your sister was hurt in the game last week. What happened?" Then listens as Peggy responds.	X
Teacher blows whistle to signal end of practice, and waits as students stop activity.	F

SAMPLE CODING FORM

TEACHER FUNCTION

CLASS: _H.S. Basketball_   TEACHER: _Jim Brown_

CODES: (I) Instructing   (C) Class management
        (M) Monitoring motor activities   (B) Behavior management
        (F) Officiating/regulating motor act.   (X) Other

5 second coding intervals (2 min)

interval	1	2	3	4	5	6	7	8	9	10
1	X	B	M	M	I	C	F	C	M	F
2		C			M		I			M
3					M,I		I			
4				C	M,I		F			
5			M,I		C		M			
6			M,I							
7			M							F
8		C,B		I			F			F
9		B		I	F		F	M	M,I	F
10		C		X			F	M,I		M
11							M		M	
12			I					F		
13	C					M		F		
14								I		
15				I		C		M		
16				I					F	
17		C		M					F	
18		C	M,I			F		M		
19		M	M,I			M				
20			I					F		
21								F		C
22								F		
23	B			I		F		M	F	
24	B		M	M		F		M	F	

NOTE: Coded first 20 minutes of class and stopped.

TOTALS: (I) Instructing: f = 27; % = $27/240$ = 11.3%
        (M) Monitoring motor activities: f = 96; % = $96/240$ = 40%
        (F) Officiating/regulating motor activities: f = 23; % = $23/240$ = 9.6%
        (C) Class management: f = 79; % = $79/240$ = 30%
        (B) Behavior management: f = 4; % = $4/240$ = 1.7%
        (X) Other: f = 17; % = $17/240$ = 7.1%

SUMMARY COMMENTS AND EVALUATION (by observed teacher)

Overall, provided too little instruction.
During game concentrated too much on officiating and too little on instructing. Took too long to get teams organized.
Preliminary practice and instruction (columns 3 + 4) was too short. Took too long to get started (column 1).

HOW AND WITH WHOM DOES THE TEACHER COMMUNICATE?

Formal education brings people together in common settings called classes because we believe that live, interactive communication between teacher and students is indispensable to effective education. All teachers are obligated to use these precious opportunities for interactive communication efficiently and skillfully. A teacher's success is likely to depend heavily on the types and methods of communication she employs.

The Clinical Tasks in this section examine the patterns of communication used by physical education teachers—particularly the "mode" of communication (talking, demonstrating, listening, etc.) and the "direction" of communication (the person[s] with whom the teacher communicates). Some of our research studies have turned up some rather interesting findings with respect to the mode and direction of communication used by physical education teachers. For example, of all the behavioral units recorded for teachers in forty physical education classes, 72% involved teacher talk exclusively or teacher talk in combination with some other mode, 13% involved listening, and only 3% involved demonstrating (Barrette, 1977); Morgenegg (1977) found that 57% of all physical education teachers' interactions were directed toward individual students, 26.8% toward the whole class, and 16.2% toward groups of students. In over four thousand instances in which eighty-two different physical education teachers gave feedback to students about their performance of a motor skill, the teacher relied exclusively on verbal feedback (i.e., no demonstration or visual message) in 95.2% of the cases (Tobey, 1974).

Analysis of communication in physical education classes is complicated by the fact that so much of the communication is done through, or in relation to, movement. While communication in regular academic classrooms is often analyzed by studying audio or written transcripts of verbal utterances only, in physical education settings words alone don't tell the story. So the approach to analysis suggested here attempts to account for the role of movement as well as words in communication.

In Clinical Task 10, you will code the mode and direction of teacher behavior simultaneously. These two dimensions have been combined in one coding operation for the sake of efficiency, and in order to produce a more meaningful record.

**Clinical Task 10—CODING THE MODE AND DIRECTION OF TEACHER
BEHAVIOR**

1. Study the category definitions, coding procedures, and coding form and record (pp. 46-48). Practice coding on a few occasions until you can do so accurately and efficiently.
2. Select a class taught by another teacher and code 2- or 3-minute samples of teacher behavior at several points in the class.
3. Compute the total frequency and percentage of time spent for both the mode and direction of teacher behavior.
4. Show the record to the teacher whose behavior was coded, and, together with that teacher, make appropriate entries under Summary Comments and Evaluation.
5. Have someone code the mode and direction of your behavior as you teach a class, then complete steps 3 and 4. Or, if you have a videotape of your own teaching performance, code it yourself.

DEFINITIONS, PROCEDURES, AND GROUND RULES FOR CODING TEACHER COMMUNICATIONS

Category definitions

MODE OF COMMUNICATION

(T) *Talks:* Conveys verbal messages by speaking.

(L) *Listens:* Attends to verbal messages from others.

(O) *Observes:* Silently attends to the behavior of other people.

(D) *Demonstrates:* Performs motor activity for the purpose of illustration.

(A) *Uses aids or assistant:* Uses audiovisual or visual aids, written materials, or student demonstrator to convey messages.

(S) *Uses signaling device:* Uses whistle, hand clap, drum, etc., to convey messages.

(M) *Manually assists:* Touches other person in a way that affects person's movement.

(P) *Participates:* Performs motor activity as participant.

(N) *Noninteractive:* Not actively communicating with or attending to students in class (e.g., tying shoes, gazing out window, talking with visitors, etc.)

DIRECTION OF COMMUNICATION

(1) *One student:* Teacher's behavior is directed toward one student.

(2) *Group of students:* Teacher's behavior is directed toward more than one student, but not the whole class.

(3) *Whole class:* Teacher's behavior is directed toward the whole class.

Coding procedures

1. Focus on the teacher's behavior and ask yourself, "How and with whom is he or she communicating?"
2. Code the teacher's behavior at the end of (approximately) every 5-second interval by placing the code letter for the appropriate "mode" category in the appropriate "direction" column. For example, when the teacher talks to the whole class, place a T in column 3. (See sample coding form and record.)
3. Enter code sequentially in a vertical column, one code per line. Use a vertical arrow to indicate a continuation of a behavior for several intervals. When you reach the bottom of the page, start a new column.
4. Make any notations you wish next to the codings to help you to recollect events that appear to be significant.
5. At the conclusion of the period, total the codings in each category/column and make appropriate entries on an "analysis table" (see sample form). Calculate the approximate percentage of time spent in each mode and direction category using:

$$\frac{\text{no. of codings for category}}{\text{no. of lines (intervals) on coding form}}$$

Make appropriate entries under Summary Comments and Evaluation.

Special procedure

If the observer knows the names of the students in the observed class, he or she can systematically note the name of each student who is the target of an individualized teacher interaction (column 1). If this procedure turns out to be too cumbersome, forget it.

Special ground rules

1. When two or more modes/directions occur during the same interval, record the appropriate multiple codes on the same line.* (NOTE: These multiple codes will tend to inflate the total percentages derived for certain categories.)
2. Place code for noninteractive (N) and participates (P) outside the directional column.
3. You will have difficulty trying to decide the "direction" of the teacher's "observation"—i.e., who the teacher is looking at. Do the best you can. Try to be consistent from one coding to the next. In any event, recognize that these data will lack reliability and interpret the results accordingly.

----

*EXCEPTION: Since "observes" and "noninteractive" will occur frequently for a moment or two in many intervals, use these codes ("O" and "N") only when an entire 5-second interval is spent either observing or in noninteractive behavior.

SAMPLE CODING FORM AND RECORD

MODE AND DIRECTION OF TEACHER BEHAVIOR

CODES

DIRECTION: (1) Individual, (2) Group, (3) Class.

MODE: (T) talks, (L) listens, (O) observes,
(D) demonstrates, (A) aids/assistants,
(S) signals, (M) manually assists,
(P) participates, (N) non-interactive.

CLASS: Elementary Volleyball
TEACHER: T. Smith

5 SECOND INTERVALS	(1)	(2)	(3)		(1)	(2)	(3)		(1)	(2)	(3)		(1)	(2)	(3)		(1)	(2)	(3)	
1		O					T		TD					O				O		
2									TD									OT		
3									TD									O		
4									TD				T				Jim			
5		T						T												
6		T						T										↓		
7			N					O										OT		
8			N										T			Jim		O		
9	T																			
10	T																			
11		T																		
12													T							
13							↓						ST							
14							T						T			↓				
15							T									OT				
16		↓						T								OT				
17	L				↓								↓			T				
18	T					O							T							
19	T			LT			O					T								
20		T		T			O					T								
21				T	T								T							
22					T															
23					T															
24		↓			T		↓						↓			↓				

NOTE: Coded five 2-minute samples.

ANALYSIS TABLE

	INDIVID.	GROUP	CLASS	TOTAL f/% *
Talks	16	21	38	83/69%
Listens	2	—	—	2/1.7%
Observes	7	30	5	42/35%
Demonstrates	—	4		4/3.4%
Uses aids	—	—	—	1/.8%
Signals	—	—	1	—
Man. assists	—	—	—	—
Participates	—	—	—	—
Non-inter.	—	—	—	2/1.7%
TOTAL f/%	25/20.2%	55/44.4%	44/35.5%	

SUMMARY COMMENTS AND EVALUATION

(by observed teacher)

I talked more than I intended to.
Paid too much attention to Jim and not to others.
Spent less time with individuals than I thought I would.
Didn't do much listening.
Should I rely on talk only, or use more demonstrating?

* % of 120 intervals coded.

WHAT IS THE TEACHER TALKING ABOUT?

Having examined the mode and direction of teacher communications, a reasonable next step is to study the *contents* of those communications. Of particular interest are the contents of instructional messages, that is, the "subject matter" of a class or course. After all, students are in school to learn about *something,* and most teachers spend much of their time trying to communicate that *something* to students.*

There has been some lively controversy of late about what constitutes the legitimate subject matter of physical education. Some persons believe that sports skills together with game rules and strategies are the central components of subject matter. Others argue for the primacy of broad concepts of movement, fitness, and health. Still others support personal-psychologic insights and understandings as key elements of content for students in physical education. Regardless of the disparity in positions, however, almost everyone acknowledges the central role of some type of subject matter in the educational process.

Clinical Task 11 involves coding the (subject matter) contents of your communications in terms of your own conception of content. The procedure is relatively simple: you identify "what" you intend to teach during a class or segment of a class; develop a list of the items of content to be covered; during the class an observer uses the list to code each reference made to each item of content and writes in other items that come up. The Sample Coding Forms and Records (p. 51) illustrate the sort of approach that might be taken.

Obviously this is a rather open-ended coding assignment. You have to decide how to identify and define an element of content (subject matter). In doing so you'll have to determine just how specific or general each listed item of content should be, and what constitutes a legitimate "reference" to that item of content. Try to keep the procedure as simple as possible; don't get caught up in an excessively detailed category system or elaborate coding procedures. The main purpose here is to obtain a meaningful record of the extent to which you emphasized the elements of content which *you believe to be crucial.*

------

*Certainly there are other sources of instructional information besides the teacher—e.g., other students, books, posters, task cards, loop films, and so on. Furthermore, the use of indirect or discovery methods of teaching often encourage students to be their own sources of information. I applaud the judicious use of these resources and methods. This section, however, is designed to focus on those segments of in-class teacher behavior when the teacher serves as the primary source of instructional information.

Clinical Task 11—CODING THE CONTENT OF THE TEACHER'S INSTRUCTION

1. Develop a set of content categories that reflect the subject matter to be covered in an upcoming class. In doing so, consult with the teacher of the class in order to identify the general and specific items of content that are likely to be covered. Leave space for "other" items of subject matter that might be mentioned (see examples of categories developed for specific classes, p. 51).

2. Code those segments of the class during which the teacher expects to cover the content.

3. Focus on the teacher's talk. Each time an item of content is mentioned, place a check next to the appropriate content category. (See Sample Coding Forms and Records, p. 51.)

4. Show the record to the teacher whose behavior was coded, and, together with the teacher, make appropriate entries under Summary Comments and Evaluation.

5. Have someone code the content of your instruction as you teach a class; then complete step 4. Or, if you have a videotape of your teaching performance, code it yourself.

SAMPLE CODING FORMS AND RECORDS

CONTENT OF TEACHER'S INSTRUCTION

A check (✓) is recorded each time the teacher refers to a listed item of content.

TENNIS LESSON ON BACKHAND DRIVE	BASIC MOVEMENT LESSON ON THROWING
1. Entire stroke (general) ✓✓	1. Performance elements
2. Grip (general) ✓	— Eyes on target ✓
— ⅛th turn ✓	— Feet apart ✓✓
— 45% angle	— Rotate trunk
— Other (list) too loose ✓	— Weight to back foot
3. Backswing (general)	— Elbow bent
— Short ✓	— Transfer weight to front foot
— Help with left hand ✓	— Point of release ✓✓
— Body pivot ✓✓✓✓✓✓✓✓✓	— Follow through ✓✓
— Elbow position ✓	2. Major concepts
— Other (list)	— Point of release affects direction
4. Forward swing (general) ✓	✓✓✓✓
— Arc of racket ✓	— Transfer of weight gives power
— Point of contact ✓✓✓✓✓✓✓✓✓	3. Common errors
— Angle of contact	— Facing front ✓✓✓✓✓✓✓✓
— Other (list) eye on ball ✓✓✓✓✓	— No rotation ✓✓✓
5. Follow through (general) ✓	— Pushing
— Racket head rises	4. Other (list)
— Topspin	forgot to snap wrist ✓✓
— Other (list) smoothness ✓	"stride" toward target ✓
6. Common errors	angle of projection ✓
— Excessive body action	
— Chopping	
— Other (list) backswing too long ✓✓	
elbow push ✓	
7. Other (list)	
getting into position ✓✓✓✓✓✓✓	
anticipating flight of ball ✓✓✓✓	
✓✓✓✓✓	

SUMMARY COMMENTS AND EVALUATION	SUMMARY COMMENTS AND EVALUATION
I neglected the "follow through."	Tried to cover too much with these
I forgot to include "eye on ball" in	third graders so purposely left out
initial plan, but covered it with	some things.
individual students.	Forgot to cover weight transfer = greater
"Positioning" and "anticipation" came up	power.
frequently, include in future presen-	Too many students had to be corrected
tations.	for facing front, emphasize sideward
Emphasized "point of contact" and	stance next time.
forgot about "angle of contact."	Performance elements were covered at
	beginning, but not during later
	practice.

MAKING CHANGES

If you are like most of us, there are probably some features of the records of your behavior that strike you as "good" or "appropriate," other features that are difficult to interpret, and some features that point to obvious deficiencies or problems. Clinical Task 12 is designed to give you an opportunity to improve your teaching by correcting perceived deficiencies or problems. Obviously the identification of needed changes will depend on the specific features of the obtained records and the judgments you choose to make about them. In assessing the records it is usually advantageous to consult with the observer or another qualified person so that at least one outside perspective can be brought to bear in making judgments.

Some of the problems commonly identified by teachers who have used the previous coding procedures are listed here. They may or may not be your problems.

I spend too little time giving instruction, and/or too much time in class management and behavior management.

I spend a lot of time monitoring student performance of motor activities but then fail to give instructional feedback based on what I've seen.

When I get involved in officiating a game I tend to forget about giving instruction.

I don't engage in enough individual interactions with students, or I don't interact with enough different individuals.

I interact frequently with the best and the worst students, but neglect the average ones.

I rely exclusively on talk as a mode of communication, when on so many occasions a demonstration would be more effective.

I spend very little time listening to students (which indicates that I don't solicit information from them as often as I'd like to).

I tend to be excessively repetitious in mentioning some items of content, and totally neglect others.

The items I emphasize in the preparatory stages of instruction I tend to forget about later, when I'm giving students feedback.

I spend too much time dealing with incidental items of content that happen to arise, and often neglect the crucial elements of content I'd planned on covering.

Clinical Task 12—USING CODINGS OF YOUR BEHAVIOR AS A BASIS FOR CHANGING TEACHING

Using the records of your own teaching behavior:
1. Review the records from Tasks 9, 10, and 11 with the observer, and ask yourselves:
   a. Which aspects of behavior are satisfactory, and which need to be changed? (Compose list.)
   b. Which *two* or *three* changes would yield the most important improvements in teaching? (You may identify generic changes needed across classes, or one type of change needed in one class and a different change needed in another class.)
2. Write out the changes identified in *b* and indicate the extent to which they should be reflected in subsequent coding records of your behavior. (If possible, set quantitative targets for the future. For example: "I would like to spend at least 50% of my time giving instruction," or "I should interact with at least fifteen different individual students during the period.")
3. Reteach the class or the lesson and have someone recode your behavior, using one or a combination of the coding procedures from Tasks 9, 10, or 11. You may wish to limit the coding procedure to only those aspects of behavior which you intend to change.
4. Analyze the extent to which you changed your behavior in the desired direction.

FOR THE ENTHUSIAST

If these descriptive records of teacher behavior yield valuable information for you, perhaps you will want to use them in different ways or vary the procedures used to obtain information better suited to your own purposes.

You may want to try some of the variations mentioned at the end of Chapter 2—i.e., developing your own category system for coding teacher behavior, combining approaches, restructuring categories, and determining objectivity of coding. In particular, you may want to obtain records of your behavior from three or four different classes to determine just how stable or variable your behavior is across classes and over time.

If you have two coders available, it can be quite revealing to obtain a record of your behavior (Task 9) and your students' behavior (Task 5) for the same class; or to intersperse spot-checks of student behavior (Task 7) while coding teacher behavior (Tasks 9 and 10).

4

Evaluating student improvement

Most teachers recognize that, while they are called upon to perform a varied array of functions, their principal responsibility is to help students learn. Obviously, then, a most important way to analyze and evaluate teaching is to examine its impact on learning.

As obvious as this course of action may be, most of us rarely undertake such an examination. Instead we too often "go through the motions" considered to be consistent with good teaching and are satisfied if we do what teachers are supposed to do—e.g., if we demonstrate properly, if we cover the material, if we provide adequate practice opportunities, and so on. In effect, we judge ourselves primarily on the *form* our actions take, rather than on their *effect* on student learning. Ironically, when we do systematically evaluate student learning, our purpose is usually to determine how well *they* are doing, not how well *we* are doing.

On those occasions when we do look to students for clues about the impact of our teaching, the examination is usually limited to our own admittedly biased and incidentally gathered *impressions* of whether students seem to be progressing— hardly a fair test of our productivity. More often than not, however, we avoid assessing ourselves on the basis of student learning and instead are content to see that students are *involved in the task,* or that they seem to be *having fun,* or even that they are *well behaved.*

Clinical Task 13 is an attempt to encourage you to use evidence of student learning as a basis for evaluating your teaching. You will be asked to:
1. Identify what you want students to learn
2. Devise a reasonably objective and valid method of measuring that learning
3. Beforehand, use the measure to find out how much students already know or are able to do
4. Teach them what you want them to learn
5. Measure their improvement (learning)
6. Use the evidence of improvement (or lack thereof) to evaluate your teaching

There are, perhaps, two essential characteristics that distinguish this approach to the analysis and evaluation of teaching. First, you will be judging yourself, not by what you do or how you do it, but by whether or not you *produce*. Second, you will not be content with vague impressions of whether the students are learning; you will rely on hard-nosed evidence of that learning.

Practice and mastery of this approach should hopefully equip you with an analytic technique that can be applied to many aspects of your teaching. Beyond this, however, if your experience corresponds with the experiences of others who have used this approach, you should discover that the task provides a marvelously refreshing opportunity to zero in on the core elements of teaching. Knowing that you are "on the line" to produce changes in students, you are likely to invent new and imaginative strategies to ensure student learning; your energies will be concentrated on helping students to improve; and, most importantly, you are likely to get an enormous boost when clear evidence of student progress emerges. At the same time, you will probably be less concerned with the routine and trivial aspects of teaching that so often clutter the scene. In short, you will find yourself fully absorbed in the real business of teaching.

SOME LIMITATIONS AND SUGGESTIONS FOR DEALING WITH THEM

As with any attempt to evaluate teaching, this approach has its limitations. In this case, the limitations are related to achieving accuracy in evaluating student learning, and to establishing cause-effect relationships between teaching and learning.

Accurate evaluation of student learning is not easy, even for experts. Any number of problems or obstacles can intervene to reduce the validity of the evaluation. For example, learning may occur but may not be detected because the measuring instruments are not sensitive enough or sufficiently refined; the method of measurement (perhaps a test) may involve such a small sample of student performance that it is an unreliable index of the students' capabilities; gauging student progress in terms of certain types of objectives (e.g., improving form in a gymnastic movement) may demand the use of relatively subjective measures (e.g., judges' ratings) which tend to lack reliability; or, for a variety of external reasons, the students may not perform up to their true capabilities in the test setting.

In completing Clinical Task 13, when you evaluate student learning, be cognizant of the problems cited above (as well as others you are familiar with), and try your best to cope with them. For example: try to use objective measures when possible; when subjective ratings are necessary, define what is to be rated as carefully as possible; try to choose measures that are sensitive to small increments in student performance; and so on. In other words, try your best to assess learning in a responsible manner, but don't go overboard. Don't spend so much time trying to perfect your measurement techniques that you lose sight of the central concern of this task, analyzing teaching. Don't let the measurement procedures become so burdensome that the whole undertaking becomes impracticable. Instead, try to strike a reasonable balance between collecting responsible evidence of student progress and maintaining a realistic teaching-learning framework. The Sample Records (pp. 58-62) illustrate the kind of balanced approach to this task that seems appropriate; they place greater emphasis on objective measurement than one is likely to find in a normal physical education setting, and yet the measurement task is kept manageable and is easily fit into the instructional setting.

Another cluster of limitations has to do with establishing cause-effect relationships between teaching and learning, or, for that matter, between any two distinct sets of phenomena. After having observed an improvement in student performance (learning), it is no simple matter to decide whether anything you did actually influenced that learning. After all, the students might have improved as a consequence of some outside influence—perhaps they practiced at home, or possibly they picked up the skill from another student, or conceivably the students disregarded your instruction and stumbled onto the improvement through their own trials and errors. Indeed, there are those who contend that in many educational settings students learn *in spite* of their teachers, not *because* of them. Even when there does seem to be an obvious connection between teaching and learning, it is often difficult to figure out which of the many teacher actions had a significant influence on the learning.

The only acknowledged way to cope with this problem is to conduct tightly controlled experiments in which specified teacher actions are systematically varied and concomitant changes in student performance are carefully monitored (and even then cause-effect relationships can only be estimated in terms of probabilities). In Clinical Task 13, you will not be able to, nor should you attempt to, set up such an experiment. To do so would only distort the natural realities of the educational setting and thus yield results that have little to do with your normal teaching procedures. Instead, you are going to have to work within the naturalistic and comparatively uncontrolled teaching-learning setting; collect some before-and-after evidence of student progress; and be content to make some *educated guesses* about the connections between your teaching and their learning.

Of course there are some things you can do to enhance the validity of the relationships you identify. For example, narrow down the focus for teaching and learning to a clearly identifiable task; make your instruction directly relevant to the desired learning; if possible, measure student performance immediately before and immediately after instruction; and so on. Nevertheless, you will still have to live with the speculative nature of any conclusions you reach about the effect of teaching on learning.

Clinical Task 13—EVALUATING STUDENT IMPROVEMENT

1. Review the classes you are now teaching and identify some of the most important kinds of improvements you would like to see occur in your students' peformance, knowledge, or attitude.
2. Narrow the list to two or three key improvements, and rank them first, second, and third.
3. Using the first ranked improvement, write out a specific objective for students that describes the type of improvement desired. At the same time develop an evaluative method for measuring (or rating) the students' progress toward the objective. (See Sample Records, pp. 58-62.) The method may involve an objective performance measure, a movement rating, a game performance measure, a knowledge test, or some other method of collecting evidence about student progress.
4. Use the evaluative method to obtain a *baseline measure* of student performance. Employ an *instructional strategy* designed to help students improve their performance in terms of the objective. Then use the same evaluative method to *measure student improvement*. (See Sample Records, pp. 58-62.)
5. Use the improvement scores (difference between baseline measure and improvement measure) as a basis for analyzing the effectiveness of the instructional strategy and making suggestions for the future.
6. Using your second ranked improvement, try the process again (steps 3 through 5). Preferably use a different type of objective and evaluative method on this second attempt.

SAMPLE RECORD

EVALUATING STUDENT IMPROVEMENT (GAME PERFORMANCE)

SETTING: *Seventh-grade class involved in a soccer unit. Have played two or three scrimmage games. Problem: Players are not advancing the ball by passing to teammates — they concentrate exclusively on dribbling and clearing.*

OBJECTIVE: *Increase the number of attempted passes during game, and the number of completed passes (successful) during game.*

BASELINE MEASURE: *Observe soccer game for 15 minutes; count "attempted passes" (i.e., player clearly attempted to pass the ball forward to open teammate); count successfully "completed passes" (i.e., ball passed forward and received by teammate).*

15 minutes of play

Team 1: *Attempted passes — 6*
Completed passes — 2

Team 2: *Attempted passes — 5*
Completed passes — 1

INSTRUCTIONAL STRATEGY: *Teacher reemphasizes importance of passing. Shows teams baseline measures of passing. Conducts passing drills. Has students play modified game in which completed pass counts as half a goal.*

IMPROVEMENT MEASURE: *Taken at beginning of subsequent class. Observe regular game for 15 minutes; count attempted and completed passes.*

15 minutes of play

Team 1: *Attempted passes — 14   (+8)*
Completed passes — 7   (+5)

Team 2: *Attempted passes — 18   (+13)*
Completed passes — 3   (+2)

ANALYSIS AND COMMENTS: *Team 1 improved in attempts and completions, and consequently improved the quality of their team's play. Some members of Team 2 got into the habit of unnecessarily passing and passing to teammates who were not open. As a result, although they did more passing it did not improve the quality of their play. I think the use of the modified game made the big difference in getting the players to attend more to passing.*

SUGGESTIONS FOR FUTURE: *Work on players' ability to distinguish appropriate/inappropriate passing situations.*

EVALUATING STUDENT IMPROVEMENT
(OBJECTIVE PERFORMANCE MEASURE)

SETTING: *Fourth-grade class involved in a unit on fundamental movement.*

OBJECTIVE: *Improve performance of selected students on standing broad jump.*

BASELINE MEASURE: *Taken at beginning of period. Record best of two jumps.*

John	4'6"	Jim	6'4"
Jane	4'5"	Mary	3'4"
Alice	5'3"	Tom	4'4"

INSTRUCTIONAL STRATEGY: *Teacher provides instruction in fundamentals of standing broad jump, emphasizing arm swing, push-off, and body position in landing. Provides eight to ten practice trials per student. Teacher diagnoses student performance and gives individualized feedback.*

IMPROVEMENT MEASURE: *Taken at end of period. Record best of two jumps.*

John	5'2"	(+8")	Jim	6'0"	(−4")
Jane	4'5"	(0")	Mary	4'4"	(+12")
Alice	5'4"	(+1")	Tom	5'0"	(+6")

ANALYSIS AND COMMENTS: *Mary and Tom improved because they used their arms more efficiently and kept their weight forward on landing. My individualized feedback about their arm position was most helpful. Not sure why John improved. Jane and Alice stayed approximately the same in distance—I was unable to get them to push off more forcefully. Jim got worse—he was probably thinking about too many things (my instructions).*

SUGGESTIONS FOR FUTURE: *Put more emphasis on diagnosis and correction of individual students' problem (Jane and Alice). Leave well enough alone (Jim).*

SAMPLE RECORD

EVALUATING STUDENT IMPROVEMENT (KNOWLEDGE TEST)

SETTING: *Eleventh-grade class in Lacrosse. Initial class meeting. Students' first exposure to Lacrosse.*

OBJECTIVE: *Students should know the basic rules of the game as evidenced by satisfactory performance on a knowledge test.*

BASELINE MEASURE: *None. Assume students do not know the rules.*

INSTRUCTIONAL STRATEGY: *Explain basic rules of the sport; use audiovisual aids. Put students in simulated game setting; use game setting to illustrate rules and violations.*

KNOWLEDGE ACQUISITION MEASURE: *At the beginning of the next class administer 10-item objective test on rules. Students score partners' tests.*

RESULTS:

Number correct	Number of students	Item number (number of incorrect student responses)	
10 ⟶	5	1 (4)	6 (4)
9 ⟶	4	2 (13)	7 (2)
8 ⟶	8	3 (0)	8 (4)
7 (Satisfactory) ⟶	3	4 (3)	9 (12)
6 ⟶	2	5 (2)	10 (15)
5 (and below) ⟶	4		

ANALYSIS AND COMMENTS: *The vast majority of the class achieved a satisfactory score. Students did poorly on items 2, 9, and 10. Either these rules were not well explained, or the test items are defective. I never did get to illustrate the rules in items 9 and 10 in the simulated game setting.*

SUGGESTIONS: *Review selected rules (items 2, 9, and 10) before proceeding. Examine test items 2, 9, and 10 for possible defects.*

SAMPLE RECORD

EVALUATING STUDENT IMPROVEMENT (MOVEMENT RATING)

SETTING: *Ninth-grade class in beginners gymnastics. Students have been practicing floor exercises. Four students are having particular difficulty mastering the cartwheel.*

OBJECTIVE: *Increase proficiency rating of selected students (4) in performance of cartwheel.*

Rating Scale for Cartwheel

(1) Did not complete task: *hand-hand-foot-foot.*
(2) Completed task at lowest level: *hand-hand-foot-foot in proper sequence.*
(3) Average: *hips and legs within 20 degrees of vertical.*
(4) Above average: *Maintains vertical position, legs split, arms extended, stable landing.*
(5) Exceptional: *Unusual extension, grace, control, soft landing, toes pointed.*

BASELINE MEASURE: *At beginning of class, record* best *rating for two trials.*

Hillary	*2*
Glen	*1*
Nick	*1*
Pat	*1*

INSTRUCTIONAL STRATEGY: *Work with each student individually for at least 5 minutes. Concentrate on diagnosing individual students' problem, providing feedback and prescribing corrections. Allow for subsequent practice.*

IMPROVEMENT MEASURE: *At end of period, record best rating for two trials.*

Hillary	*3 (+1)*
Glen	*2 (+1)*
Nick	*1 (0)*
Pat	*3 (+2)*

ANALYSIS AND COMMENTS: *Hillary improved verticality after I manually assisted her. Emphasis on "straight arm position" helped Glen and Pat. In general, use of the "part method" of teaching (arms, hips, legs) seemed to help all three. Nick's arms keep collapsing.*

SAMPLE RECORD

EVALUATING STUDENT IMPROVEMENT (AFFECTIVE/INTERVIEW)

SETTING: *Second-grade class involved in ball skills phase of basic movement program. Some students appear to be both disinterested and poorly skilled.*

OBJECTIVE: *Identify students who perform poorly, have a poor image of their capabilities, and dislike the activity. Attempt to improve their images of their capabilities and their liking for the activity.*

BASELINE MEASURE: *On an individual basis, ask selected students:*

	Jane	John	Lynn
Do you like ball activities?	*No*	*Yes*	*Unsure*
Are you good at ball activities?	*No*	*No*	*No*
Do you think you can get better?	*Unsure*	*Yes*	*No*

INSTRUCTIONAL STRATEGY: *Intermittently, during the next two classes, work with Jane and Lynn. Provide easier tasks; use larger balls; provide for graduated progression; play with them; praise their improvement; invent "fun games" for them; and, in general, show an interest in them.*

IMPROVEMENT MEASURE: *Two or three days later, ask the same questions:*

	Jane	Lynn
Do you like ball activities?	*No*	*Yes*
Are you good at ball activities?	*No*	*Unsure*
Do you think you can get better?	*Unsure*	*Yes*

ANALYSIS AND COMMENTS: *It seems to have worked with Lynn. Not only did she respond better to the questions, but her enthusiasm in class is noticeably improved. I think the key to her success was in starting with easier tasks. Jane has not shown much change—try something else. (Recognize the possibility that ball skills may simply not be attractive to Jane.)*

FOR THE ENTHUSIAST
Extending the time for learning

Most of the examples on the previous pages deal with short-term student learning—i.e., learning that occurs and can be observed within a class period or two. This limitation has been purposeful; by keeping the target learning within a confined period of time, you have a better chance of identifying the elements of your teaching that were responsible for the change in student behavior. Obviously, however, much student learning does not show itself within the space of a period or even two or three. It can take weeks or months for students to demonstrate progress in some complex skills (sometimes it seems to take forever); or it can take an entire semester to have a noticeable impact on a student's attitude toward an activity.

Recognizing the need to allow more time for student improvement to accrue, you may wish to complete a version of Clinical Task 13 that allows more time between the baseline measure and the improvement measure—perhaps a week, or the time it takes to complete a unit, or a semester. In doing so, make sure that the student spends appreciable portions of the elapsed time on the target learnings or tasks, and be certain that your teaching strategy is consistently applied over time to produce the desired improvement. This approach may allow you to see results that otherwise would be obscured—i.e., what you were unable to produce in a day or two, you may be able to produce in a week.

In extending the time for learning, however, recognize that the relationship between particular aspects of instruction and the learning that takes place will be even more difficult to establish. A lot of things happen during 3 or 4 weeks of instruction (including events outside of class), and so it's not easy to pin down the particular combination of things that led to the observed improvement.

Using student feedback to identify relationships between teaching and learning

Like most of us, you probably have difficulty identifying the factors that contributed to student improvement. Why not get some help? Ask the students to identify the factors that they believe were most crucial to their success. After all, the students did the improving—they are in at least as good a position as you are to figure out why they improved. You may even want to ask those who failed to progress to explain why they didn't improve, although it is especially difficult to isolate crucial reasons for failure because the possibilities are so enormous.

If you work with only a few students, the simplest way to obtain feedback is to question them directly after the improvement occurs. If you need to obtain information from a relatively large group of students or from the whole class, then try using a version of written *informal analysis by students* (p. 14). You might even ask for the feedback in the form of *critical incidents* (p. 19)—i.e., ask them to describe the incidents they believe responsible for their improvement.

Time out

For some people the analysis of teaching can be hectic. They move so rapidly from one clinical task to the next, there is no time to digest what they have learned, or to carry out the changes they want to make. Others, feeling overwhelmed by the mounting paper work required, yearn for a return to the simpler life, just plain teaching. Still others, puzzled by the seemingly disparate sets of information collected thus far, can't seem to get a coherent overall picture of their teaching performance or progress.

If one or more of these problems confront you, take a break (perhaps a week or two) before moving on to the next Clinical Task.

In the interim, do whatever makes the most sense for you. Certainly a viable option would be to return to your normal teaching routine. Aside from providing a refreshing change of pace, this might allow you to catch up on matters that have been neglected while you were enmeshed in analysis.

If you started to work on certain changes in your teaching and need more time to refine those changes, by all means do so. This time don't bother with observers, formal analysis, or record keeping; just do it.

If you are having trouble integrating the information already collected, try some quiet reflection. Look over the accumulated records. Think about the relationships among the data. Consider the similarities between your evaluative comments. Try to determine how the records reflect (or fail to reflect) your beliefs about teaching. If possible, discuss the whole matter with colleagues, preferably someone who has been through this process. You may even want to glance ahead at Chapter 8; it provides some structured guidance for "putting the pieces together."

At this stage of your work you are familiar with, and able to use, a variety of analytic techniques. Can you identify those techniques? Do you understand their strengths and limitations? Do you have ideas about how they might be used in the future? If not, it may be worthwhile to review what you already know about the analysis of teaching.

A RETURN TO INFORMAL OBSERVATION

One of the more revealing things you might do during this time-out period is to return to informal observation and analysis. Simply watch a class in the natural, unplanned way you did originally. Don't even bother taking notes. You'll probably find it a pleasant relief to casually watch what happens, without having to concentrate on certain behaviors, fill in coding forms, and so on. More importantly, you are likely to discover that your "natural" approach to observation and analysis is not what it used to be. Your attention will be drawn to things you used to overlook. You will be more sensitive to what you are able to see and not see. Your evaluative judgments may be less profuse and of a different character. In a nutshell, your view of teaching may have changed, perhaps permanently.

5

Evaluating the quality of teacher behavior

Teacher behavior has a qualitative dimension of its own, apart from its apparent effect on students. A teacher can demonstrate a skill correctly or incorrectly; explain a concept accurately or erroneously; treat students with respect or demean them; choose an appropriate or inappropriate task for students to practice; and so on.

One approach to the evaluation and improvement of teaching is to focus directly on the behaviors exhibited by teachers, try to assess the quality of those behaviors, and then use the assessment as a basis for improving future performance; this approach is used in this chapter.

A qualified observer will use an evaluation form to guide his observation of your teaching. In effect, he will look directly at what you do, and try to judge how well you did it. This represents a distinct departure from previous Clinical Tasks, in which the focus for observation was a quantitative description of teacher or student behavior, or a determination of student improvement. It should enable us to focus on qualitative features of teaching that have not been dealt with in previous Clinical Tasks—so we hope to *supplement,* not replicate, previous analyses.

The focus for this direct evaluation of teacher behavior (Clinical Task 14) will be the teacher's *instructional behavior*—i.e., those behaviors that are intended to directly influence students' learning of the subject matter of physical education. If you wish to pursue this method of evaluation further, subsequent evaluations of the teacher's *managerial or interpersonal behavior* may be undertaken (see For the Enthusiast, p. 71).

Observing teacher behavior and making an immediate judgment regarding its quality is an exceedingly difficult and risky business. Even when it's done well, the process is highly subjective; when it's done poorly, the consequences can be disastrous. Nevertheless, the only way to get at several important qualitative features of teacher behavior is to judge them directly. And if the process is carefully planned, intelligently carried out, and done with an awareness of the limitations inherent in this approach, it can yield invaluable feedback.

CHOOSING THE OBSERVER

The observer should be a competent physical educator and, to the extent possible, should have experience in observing and assessing teacher performance. If you (the teacher) are enrolled in student teaching and already working under the supervision of a cooperating teacher and/or a college supervisor, then the choice of observer has already been made for you. If you are an in-service teacher and/or in a position to choose your own observer, try to choose someone who (1) has the background necessary to make expert judgments, (2) is genuinely interested in teaching and in assisting you, and (3) is courageous enough to make negative judgments when called for, but sufficiently open-minded to see beyond his or her own established preferences.

By the way, it would be advisable for the observer to read this chapter and to be familiar with other Clinical Tasks already completed.

JUDGING QUALITY

"Quality of teacher behavior" can be conceived of in a variety of ways. For purposes of this evaluation, let's think of quality as having two major dimensions: proficiency and appropriateness.

Proficiency refers to how well you do whatever you have chosen to do. For example: Did you demonstrate the movement correctly? Was the rule explained clearly? Did you accurately diagnose the student's problem?

Appropriateness refers to the extent to which your choice of behavior was appropriate for the circumstances. For example: Was the task you chose for students too easy/difficult for them? Did you intervene to correct student performance at the right time? Were the practice drills you used appropriate for the facilities and equipment available?

The evaluative approach used here (see Evaluation Form, pp. 72-73) encourages the observer to judge selected teaching behaviors on the basis of both their proficiency and appropriateness, recognizing that a proficiently executed behavior is not always appropriate, and vice versa. In effect the observer will be asked to judge whether selected behaviors are "acceptable" in terms of several component qualities of proficiency and appropriateness (e.g., accuracy, clarity, etc.). When, in the judgment of the observer, the behavior satisfies the requisite qualities, it is judged "acceptable." When it fails to satisfy one or more of the qualities, it is judged "deficient."

Furthermore, the approach used here emphasizes the identification of the "evidence" used to arrive at the judgments—the intent, if you will, is to hold the observer accountable for his judgments. The observer is required to note the specific instance(s) of teacher behavior that led to the judgment and, in the case of deficient instances, to note the nature of the deficiency. I hope this procedure will encourage observers to make judgments only about those things for which they have collected relevant evidence and will produce the kind of specific record that serves as useful feedback for teachers.*

RECOGNIZING THE LIMITATIONS

In the final analysis, the qualitative judgments made here will be subjective. Although they will be based on evidence, the observer will decide what constitutes relevant evidence. The observer will have to interpret the qualities—i.e., when a teacher's explanation is clear enough to be judged "clear," or when a choice of student activity is appropriate enough to be "appropriate," and so on. One observer's selection of evidence and interpretation of qualities is not likely to correspond with another observer's.

Judgments regarding appropriateness are particularly demanding. To judge the appropriateness of a teacher's selection of behavior is, in effect, to judge what was done in relation to what might have been done. This means that the observer must judge the chosen behavior in relation to the array of alternative behaviors available to the teacher at that point in time. It's difficult enough for the observer to "conjure up" the array of legitimate alternatives available, let alone to make judgments about how well the chosen behavior compares with those alternatives.

It is important to enter into this qualitative evaluation of teaching with a healthy respect for its imprecision and subjectivity. In this way perhaps neither the teacher nor the observer will attach unwarranted significance or validity to all of the judgments made. It is after all only one of many ways to look at and judge teaching—a way that encourages one professional to use his or her expertise and opinion to judge the behavior of another professional within a structured evaluative framework.

---

*This approach is in direct contrast with some traditional rating procedures, which often yield vague numerical ratings that are not referenced to a particular set of behaviors or events.

Clinical Task 14—EVALUATING THE QUALITY OF INSTRUCTIONAL BEHAVIOR

1. Study the Directions for Using the Evaluation Form for Instructional Behavior, pp. 69-71, and the Evaluation Form and Sample Record, pp. 72-73.
2. Discuss with the observer the kinds of evidence that will be used to make judgments on each of the items on the form.
3. Teach one or more classes while the observer uses the form to evaluate and record your behavior.
4. Discuss the results of the evaluation with the observer and identify areas of needed improvement.
5. Reteach a similar class in which the observer reevaluates your behavior to determine whether the improvements were made.

DIRECTIONS FOR USING THE EVALUATION FORM FOR INSTRUCTIONAL BEHAVIOR
Prior to the observation

1. *The teacher and observer should review the items included on the Evaluation Form (pp. 72-73), revise or delete inappropriate items, and add items they believe to be appropriate.* Don't feel obligated to judge teaching on the grounds I've suggested. It's more important that the items used reflect your own conception of the important elements of good teaching.

2. *In revising or adding items, the teacher and observer should make sure they refer to "observable behaviors" so that appropriate evidence can be collected.*

3. *The teacher and observer should discuss and agree on the types of behaviors that will be used to make judgments on each item.* The intent of this procedure is to clarify the kinds of evidence that will be used to make judgments. In doing so, it's useful to discuss specific examples of "clearly acceptable" and "deficient" instances.

4. *The teacher and observer should determine the number of classes and the portions of each class to be observed.* The intent should be to collect a reasonable amount of evidence on each of the items on the form, perhaps five to ten instances per item. This may require two or more class observations. For the sake of efficiency, it may also be wise to restrict the observation to those segments of class time during which instructional behaviors will be concentrated.

During the observation

5. *For any given time period, the observer should concentrate on collecting evidence relative to a limited number of items (perhaps three or four); then focus on a different set of items during a subsequent time period.* It's virtually impossible for an observer to keep eight or ten evaluative items in his mind at one time and try to use them all at once to judge teacher behavior. Attempts to do so usually end up in confusion or in neglecting some of the items altogether. Keeping only three or four items in mind during a particular time period allows the observer to focus on evidence related to each of them.

6. *The observer should search for "observable behaviors" that clearly represent the type of behavior referred to in the item(s).* Try to concentrate on what the teacher does, not on what he or she didn't do, or could have done, or on what you would have done. After all, at any moment in time a teacher could conceivably do any number of different things. The evaluation process can become grossly unfair if the observer constantly searches for the infinite number of things that didn't happen.

7. *When the observed behavior "clearly" satisfies "all" of the qualities listed for the behavior, record a check (✔) under "clearly acceptable instances" and add a notation that helps you to identify the particular instance (see Sample Record, pp. 72-73).* The emphasis here is on being reasonably certain that the observed

behavior was both proficiently executed and appropriate for the circumstances— i.e., that it was well done.

Judging how much teacher behavior constitutes a unit of behavior (and therefore deserves a check [✔]) cannot be easily standardized, and thus will have to depend largely on the observer's discretion. In any case, try to record a check for what you consider to be a logical unit of behavior, such as one teacher demonstration of skill, one intervention to correct a particular aspect of a student's performance, one verbal interchange between teacher and student about a particular topic, or the teacher's organization of one segment of student practice.

Some items on the form may refer to behavior that does not occur in a conveniently limited time frame, especially when several separately occurring behaviors must be viewed together to assess performance on the item. (See, for example, item 5, which refers to the teacher's structuring of the sequence of learning activities.) In these cases, an entire series of behaviors will have to be regarded as a unit.

8. *When the observed behavior clearly fails to satisfy one or more of the qualities listed for the behavior, record a check (✔) under "deficient instances" and add a notation that helps you to identify the particular instance and the nature of the deficiency (see Sample Record, pp. 72-73).* Judge the behavior as "deficient" only when you are reasonably sure that it has failed to satisfy the quality in some important way. Try not to be too picky. Remember, this is not a game to see how many holes the observer can shoot in the teacher's performance; it's an attempt to identify important and legitimate deficiencies that, if corrected, could markedly improve teacher behavior.

9. *Concentrate on observing teacher behavior, but use related student behavior as evidence for making evaluative judgments when appropriate.* In many instances, you will be able to make judgments by focusing exclusively on the teacher's behavior and comparing it to some qualitative standard, such as when you judge the correctness of a demonstration or the accuracy of a statement. In many other instances, however, you'll have to be aware of concomitant student behavior in order to make sensible judgments, such as whether the teacher has suggested an appropriate way of correcting a student's mistake.

In addition, you may want to use student responses as corroborating evidence to support your direct judgments of teacher behavior. For example, if the teacher gives directions that you think are unclear, the confused reactions of students which follow may be used to support your suspicion. But try to avoid basing your judgments primarily on the apparent effect that the teacher's behavior had on students—you've already done several evaluations of this type (see Chapter 4).

10. *When for any reason you are unsure of whether the observed behavior satisfies or fails to satisfy the qualities listed, forget about it.* It's hard enough to

make accurate judgments about those things you are reasonably certain of; don't add to the problem by forcing yourself to judge those things you are not sure of.

Procedurally, this means that many of the instructional behaviors exhibited by the teacher are not going to be a part of the evaluative record. That's alright. This evaluation is not an attempt to record everything a teacher does. It is an attempt to make legitimate value judgments based on the most usable evidence available.

11. *When a teacher omits a behavior that is clearly called for under the existing circumstances, note the omission in the space provided at the bottom of the form (see Sample Record, pp. 72-73).* Limit yourself to recording only the more blatant omissions, the kind that most any qualified outside observer might notice. Try to avoid identifying as omissions the "better ways" of doing what was done.

FOR THE ENTHUSIAST

After having been on the receiving end of this direct evaluation, you may find yourself yearning to do some evaluating of your own. If so, why not try it? Find a colleague who is willing to be evaluated and, together, repeat Clinical Task 14—this time you serve as the observer/evaluator. This should help to sharpen your capacity to critically analyze teaching; undoubtedly, it will also help you to appreciate the difficulties involved in direct evaluation of teacher behavior.

If Clinical Task 14 yielded valuable feedback about the quality of your instructional behavior, you may wish to extend this approach to focus on other dimensions of your teaching—perhaps your performance of *managerial* functions, or your *interpersonal interactions* with students, or some other aspect of your teaching that you consider crucial. In this case, all you have to do is construct an evaluation form which designates the appropriate target behaviors and their component qualities, and then proceed as you did in completing Clinical Task 14.

EVALUATION FORM FOR INSTRUCTIONAL BEHAVIOR (INCLUDING SAMPLE RECORD)

CLASS: _10th grade Softball_ _____ TEACHER: _Susan Benson_

1. Describes or explains concepts, skills, rules or strategies to be learned.

qualities	acceptable instances	deficient instances
clear, concise, accurate, appropriate for students' level, other_____ _____	✓ (batting stance) ✓ (bat position) ✓ (double play) ✓ (infielder's position)	✓ (tag-up rule unclear)

2. Provides demonstration of movements to be learned (i.e., teacher demonstration, pupil demonstration, other visual aid).

qualities	acceptable instances	deficient instances
accurate, appropriate for students, accompanied by appropriate explanation, other_____ _____	✓✓ (double play pivot) ✓ (first baseman's footwork) ✓✓✓ (batting stance and swing)	✓ (glove position too high for fielding ground ball)

3. Diagnoses student performance and intervenes to improve student performance.

qualities	acceptable instances	deficient instances
accurately identifies errors-- or effective features, suggests appropriate corrections, other_____ _____	✓ (eye on ball) ✓✓ (level swing) ✓ (grip on bat) ✓ (second baseman's stance) ✓ (rounding first base)	

4. Solicits instructional information from students (via questions or problem setting).

qualities	acceptable instances	deficient instances
clear, sufficiently focused, appropriate for students, other_____ _____		✓ (question on cut-off strategy — too general) ✓ (question on run-down technique — too difficult) ✓ (question on bunting strategy — too vague)

5. Selects and structures the sequence of learning activities.

qualities	acceptable instances	deficient instances
learning activities are: appropriate for students, logically sequenced, appropriate for available space and facilities, effectively related to one another, other_____	✓✓✓(batting slow pitched, then fast pitched balls) ✓✓(fielding ground balls)	✓(double play technique too advanced for students) ✓✓(fielding flys — too difficult) ✓(cut-off strategy — too complicated)

6. Provides opportunities for student practice of tasks/skills to be learned.

qualities	acceptable instances	deficient instances
appropriate quantity of practice, practice conditions optimal for learning, other_____	✓(throw and catch) ✓(batting practice) ✓(fielding ground balls) ✓(playing infield positions)	✓(base running practice — not realistic)

7. (add item)
   Motivates students to learn skills.

qualities	acceptable instances	deficient instances
enthusiastic, gives reasons for learning skills	✓(enthusiastic introduction of activity) ✓(explained importance of fielding)	

8. (add item)

qualities	acceptable instances	deficient instances

Omissions (Record omissions that were clearly called for under the existing circumstances.)

Did not explain how to time the pitched ball.
Did not enforce rule on bat-throwing.

6

Analyzing teacher-student interaction

Teaching is not merely acting. Actors play a part; follow the script; perform *for* the audience, not *with* it. As teachers we surely do our share of acting; but much beyond this, we *interact*. We *act* to influence the behavior of students and we *react* to what they do. The students, in turn, do their own acting and reacting to us. In a very real sense we are engaged with our audience in a series of mutually dependent actions. And, although we sometimes fail to recognize it, they influence what we do as much as we influence what they do. We ask them questions, they answer. They ask us questions, we answer. We ask them to do something, they do it, we compliment them. We ask them to do something else, they don't do it, we correct or perhaps reprimand them. We ask them to try something, they can't do it, we have them switch to something easier.

The manner in which a teacher interacts with students shapes the character and quality of the educational process. For example, some teachers spend a lot of time telling their students precisely what to do, and their students spend a lot of time doing what they are told; other teachers spend time asking their students what they want to do, and their students spend time deciding. Some teachers ask students to think about what they are doing, others merely ask them to do it—and the students respond accordingly. Some teachers react to the things students do well, others react only to student mistakes, and still others don't react at all. Some teachers respond patiently to student questions, others respond abruptly, and in some classes students don't ask questions.

The significance of a particular type of interaction extends beyond its immediate impact on a student or teacher. Forms of interaction can be self-perpetuating and thus grow into persistent patterns of interacting—patterns that, once established, are not easily broken. For example, teachers who provide all the answers for students develop students who wait for the teacher to give the answers. The more they wait, the more the teacher is obliged to continue to provide the answers, even on those occasions when the teacher wants the student to come up with the answer. In effect, teachers and students learn to play complementary interactive roles, and as each plays a role it encourages the other to continue to play a complementary role.

The Clinical Tasks in this chapter involve coding selected aspects of teacher-student interaction. In Clinical Task 15, you will code three broad types of interactive behaviors (*soliciting, responding,* and *reacting*) which should help you to see more clearly the types of interactive roles played by teachers and students. Subsequent tasks deal with a detailed examination of soliciting behaviors (Task 16) and reacting behaviors (Task 17), which will give you an opportunity to study the kinds of requests you make of students and the way you react to what they do. Task 18 focuses on your interactions with individuals. If you've never before studied interactive behaviors in an objective manner, don't be surprised to find that the realities are quite different from your prior notions of how you behave toward students. Surprised or not, you will have an opportunity to change the way you interact (Clinical Task 19) should there be reason to do so.

Before you move on to the Tasks, may I suggest that if you can possibly manage to get a videotape of one of the classes you teach, this would be the time to do it. You would be able to use and reuse the tape in completing all three Clinical Tasks and it would provide the kind of detailed record that would enable you to closely examine your particular style of interacting. If you do tape a class, try to make it a typical example of your normal teaching behavior and not a contrived performance; that way, you will get a more truthful picture of the way you relate to students and be in a better position to decide whether you want to change. If you don't have access to a videotape, don't worry; all tasks can be completed using live observation and coding.

INTERACTIVE BEHAVIORS: SOLICITING, RESPONDING, AND REACTING

Researchers have devised an enormous variety of different systems for analyzing teacher-student interaction. (See Simon and Boyer, 1970, for a summary of a sample of these systems.) One of the more elegant approaches was developed by Bellack (1966) and his co-workers to analyze verbal exchanges between teacher and students in classrooms. Their examination of transcripts of classroom discourse led to the identification of four categories of interaction (called pedagogical moves) which served as the central feature of a more elaborate system of analysis. The pedagogical moves include: *structuring,* which serves the purpose of "focusing attention on subject matter or classroom procedures and launching interactions between students and teachers"; *soliciting,* which involves eliciting a verbal or physical response from other persons, or encouraging others to attend to something; *responding,* which includes actions that fulfill the expectations of a solicitation; and *reacting,* which are moves that are occasioned, but not directly elicited, by other moves. A typical classroom interaction sequence might be categorized as follows: Teacher announces topic for lesson (structuring), asks students a question (soliciting), a student answers the question (responding), and the teacher comments on the student's answer (reacting).

Bellack used these pedagogical moves to describe the interaction in high school social studies classes. Subsequently several other researchers have used the same system to investigate interactive patterns in other educational settings. The findings of most of these studies conform rather closely to Bellack's original findings, which indicate that teachers and students play very distinctive roles in classrooms. The teacher does virtually all of the structuring. The teacher's most frequent move is to solicit responses from students and then, once the student has responded, to react to the response, usually by showing approval or disapproval. The students, for their part, engage mostly in responding to teacher solicitations. They keep their own solicitations to a minimum and usually restrict them to procedural matters. Students almost never engage in structuring and rarely react; most especially they don't react evaluatively to what the teacher says.

Morgenegg (1978) used a variation of Bellack's system to study interactive patterns in forty different physical education classes. Like the earlier classroom studies, his results show dramatic differences in the pedagogical moves of teachers as compared to those of students. Of all the structuring moves, teachers performed 75.6% and students 24.4%; teachers did 91.6% of the soliciting, students did only 8.4%. Similarly, teachers dominated the reacting moves 87.3% to 12.7% for students. On the other hand, of all the responding moves, the students were responsible for 92.7% and the teachers for 7.3%. Unlike the results for classroom studies, Morgenegg's findings show that interaction in the gymnasium focuses on movement. In most instances, teachers solicit movements, students respond by moving, and teachers react to the movement responses.

Clinical Task 15 asks you to code interactive behaviors in a physical education class and to have someone code the interaction in your class using some of Bellack's or Morgenegg's categories. To make things a bit easier, you will be asked to code only soliciting, responding, and reacting moves. Structuring moves will not be included. The results of the coding should reveal the prevalent interactive patterns in those classes, together with the types of roles played by teachers and students. This initial analysis of interaction will set the stage for subsequent Clinical Tasks, in which you take a closer look at teacher solicitations and reactions.

Clinical Task 15—CODING TEACHER-STUDENT INTERACTION

1. Study the category definitions, coding procedures, and coding form and record (pp. 78-80). Practice coding on a few occasions until you can do so accurately and efficiently. In completing this Task, simply enter appropriate codes in a vertical column (as shown on Sample Coding Form and Record); *do not* try to write out what the teacher says or does.
2. Select a class taught by another teacher and code 4- or 5-minute samples of teacher-student interaction at several points in the class.
3. Compute the total frequencies for the various categories. (See Sample Coding Form and Record, p. 80.)
4. Show the record to the teacher who taught the class and, together with the teacher, make appropriate entries under Summary Comments and Evaluation.
5. Have someone code your interactions with students as you teach a class, then complete steps 3 and 4. Or if you have a videotape of your own teaching performance, code it yourself.

DEFINITIONS AND PROCEDURES

Category definitions

Soliciting: A direction or question designed to elicit a physical or verbal response from another person (see examples p. 79).

Responding: A verbal or physical response that fulfills the expectation of the solicitation (see examples p. 79).

Reacting: An unsolicited reaction to what someone else says or does—usually involves accepting, rejecting, modifying, or expanding on what was done. Reacting moves differ from responding moves: a response is always directly elicited by a solicitation, while preceding moves serve only as the occasion for a reaction (Bellack and others, 1966). (See examples p. 79.)

Coding procedures

1. Follow the teacher and focus on the interactions that take place between teacher and students—i.e., when the teacher solicits, responds to, or reacts to the student(s); or when the student(s) solicits, responds to, or reacts to the teacher. (For purposes of this analysis, disregard teacher and student actions that do not fall into one of the three interactive categories such as lecturing, demonstrating, observing, etc. Also, focus on the teacher and whichever student he/she is interacting with—don't try to capture student-student interactions.)

2. When a solicitation occurs, code it in the appropriate column (see Sample Coding Form and Record, p. 80), indicating who did the soliciting, teacher (*T*) or student (*S*). In the same row, code the response elicited by the solicitation by indicating who responded (*T* or *S*) and the type of responses: *v* = verbal, *m* = motor activity, *o* = other behavior. If there is an immediate reaction to the response, code it in the same row. Record each subsequent solicitation and its related response and reaction in a new row.

3. In some instances an interaction will be initiated by a reaction to an ongoing event or behavior. In these cases, code the reaction by indicating who did the reacting (*T* or *S*) and what the person reacted to (*v, m, o*).

4. Code for a 4- or 5-minute period, then rest for a few minutes, and then code for another 4 or 5 minutes. Try to get a reasonable sample of the interactions that take place during a class period, perhaps four 5-minute coding periods.

5. Try to record all of the interactions that take place during a coding period, but don't be upset if things happen so quickly that you are unable to account for some of the interactions; do the best you can.

EXAMPLES OF CODING TEACHER-STUDENT INTERACTION

Codes: (T) Teacher, (S) Student, (m) Motor activity, (v) Verbal action or response, (o) Other behavior

	Solicit	Respond	React
Teacher says: "Everyone go to your places on the mats." Students go to their places.	T	So	
Teacher explains what the class will do this period.		(not coded)	
Teacher says: "Okay, Johnny, I want you to try a front walkover." Johnny attempts walkover. Teacher says: "Good try."	T	Sm	T
Teacher goes to where Diane is practicing a round-off and says: "You are not keeping your arms firm enough."			Tm
Teacher says: "Please stop talking over there." Students stop.	T	So	
Kevin asks the teacher: "Which hand should I put down first?" Teacher says: "The right one."	S	Tv	
Teacher asks Bruce: "Where are your hands supposed to be in the head stand?" "Bruce says: "Shoulder width apart." Teacher says: "Okay."	T	Sv	T
Teacher approaches Mary, who is doing a head stand, and says: "Straighten your legs." Mary tries to straighten them.	T	Sm	
Teacher blows whistle, signaling students to stop activity. Students stop. Teacher says: "That's good."	T	So	T

SAMPLE CODING FORM AND RECORD

TEACHER- STUDENT INTERACTION

CLASS: Jr. H.S. Archery   TEACHER: Dick Martin

SOLICIT	RESPOND	REACT
T	S_O	
T	S_O	
T	S_O	T
S	T_V	
T	S_M	
T	S_M	
T	S_M	T
T	S_M	T
		T_M
		T_M
T	S_O	T
T	S_M	
T	S_M	
T	S_M	
T	S_V	
T	S_M	T
		T_M
S	T_V	
T	S_M	
T	S_M	
T	S_M	T
		T_M
		T_M
		T_M
T	S_O	
T	S_O	
T	S_V	
T	S_M	T
T	S_M	
T	S_M	T
T	S_M	
T	S_M	
		T_M
		T_M
S	T_O	
T	S_M	
T	S_M	
T	S_M	
T	S_O	
T	S_O	

CODES: (T) Teacher, (S) Student
(M) Motor activity
(V) Verbal activity or response
(O) Other behavior

TOTALS:

SOLICITATIONS: 32					
By teacher: 29			By students: 3		
of verb.	mot.	oth.	of verb.	mot.	oth.
2	19	8	2	1	0

RESPONSES: 32					
By teacher: 3			By students: 29		
to verb.	mot.	oth.	to verb.	mot.	oth
2	0	1	2	19	8

REACTIONS: 16					
By teacher: 16			By students: 0		
to verb.	mot.	oth.	to verb.	mot.	oth.
0	15	1	0	0	0

MOST COMMON PATTERNS: $T \rightarrow S_M = 13$
$T \rightarrow S_M \rightarrow T = 6$
$T \rightarrow S_O = 8$
$T_M = 8$

SUMMARY COMMENTS AND EVALUATION (by observed teacher)

I do virtually all the soliciting and reacting; the students do almost all the responding

I focus on eliciting student motor responses — which is OK — but I virtually never elicit verbal responses from students — which is not OK

I seem to be reasonably conscientious about reacting to what students do

Overall, I'm concerned that I seem to start (solicit) and end (react) all the interactions

A CLOSER LOOK AT SOLICITATIONS

Teachers' solicitations tell students what they are expected to do. In most classes, where the words of the teacher are respected and followed, the students do what they are asked to do. It should be no surprise then that teacher solicitations have a powerful influence on student actions. Furthermore, in physical education classes, teachers do a great deal of soliciting—63% of all teacher actions (moves) are classified as soliciting, which makes an average of 167 solicitations per class period (Morgenegg, 1978).

Clinical Task 16 asks you to keep a verbatim record of teacher solicitations for a selected class; then analyze and evaluate that record.

Clinical Task 16—TEACHER SOLICITATIONS OF STUDENT RESPONSES

1. Observe a class taught by another teacher. Try to write down what the teacher says (verbatim) each time he or she *solicits* a response from students. Teacher solicitations include all those things coded as soliciting in Clinical Task 15. To help interpret the record, you may add notations about: what the teacher was soliciting, whether important gestures and signals were used, the tone of the solicitation, etc. (See Sample Record: Teacher Solicitations, p. 82.)

   If the teacher's solicitations are profuse, you may have difficulty getting all the words down; don't be concerned if you miss a few solicitations. If necessary, rest for a few minutes, then begin again.

2. Show the record to the teacher who taught the class and, together with the teacher, make appropriate entries under Summary Comments and Evaluation. Review the Questions to Ask about Teacher Solicitations and use them selectively in your analysis of the record.

3. Have someone keep a record of your solicitations as you teach a class, then complete step 2. Or if you have a videotape of your own teaching performance, review the tape and compose a written record of your solicitations; you should be able to do so easily because you will be able to stop it and replay sections whenever necessary.

SAMPLE RECORD

TEACHER SOLICITATIONS

CLASS: Junior high school basketball   TEACHER: Ms. Rhodes

CODES: S = Student; T = Teacher

1. "Take your spots."
2. "Everybody with no sneakers, sit on the stage."
3. T leads calisthenics.
4. "Stand up, face front."
5. "Twenty jumping jacks, ready, begin."
6. "Hands on waist, toe touches, ready, begin."
7. "Stop."
8. "Hands behind head, knee bends, ready, begin."
9. "Face the stage, sitting position, sit-up, ready, begin, and stop."
10. "Hands over head, leg lifts, ready, begin."

11. "Everybody sit on the red line."
12. "Count off by sixes."
13. "Number ones, over here; number twos, over there; number threes, over there" (etc.). (getting organized for basketball relay)
14. "One person from squad come over and get a ball."
15. "Frank, are you ready to start?"
16. "Go!" (begins relay)
17. "Get back in line." (relay in progress)
18. "Sit down when you finish."
19. "Elise, please sit."
20. "Sit down, sit down."

— — — — — — — — — — — Later in period — — — — — — — — — — —

21. "Everyone practice at least 5 lay-ups." (T had demonstrated proper lay-up)
22. S practicing lay-ups and foul shots at several different baskets.
23. "Did you take off on the correct foot?"
24. "Which foot did you take off on?" (S answers)
25. "Try it again, this time on the right foot."
26. "Hey, over there, stop fooling around."
27. "Are you using the backboard?" (S says "No")
28. "Why is it better to use the backboard?" (S answers)
29. "Try it this time on the backboard."

30. "Try it with more arc this time." (foul shot)
31. "Concentrate on the front rim."
32. "Move over here; now try it." (foul shot)
33. "Think about how the ball has to come down through the basket, and shoot it high." (foul shot)
34. "Higher this time."
35. T blows whistle; students stop.
36. "Quiet! Stop that!" (Jim fighting)
37. "Who can demonstrate a good foul shot? Mike." (Mike demonstrates)
38. "Did the ball go on a line or in an arc?" (Students answer; discussion continues)

SUMMARY COMMENTS AND EVALUATION

Do I really have to lead seventh-graders by the nose through those exercises?
Did a pretty good job of trying to get the kids to figure out what they were doing right or wrong in the lay-ups and foul shots.
Too many organizational directions in first part of period; appropriately reduced later on.
The questions asked reflect emphasis on basic concepts ("arc," use of backboard) — good.
Overall, they seem to be thinking about what they are doing (judging from their answers).

Questions to ask about teacher solicitations

Once you have obtained the record of teacher solicitations, you'll have to decide what to make of it. No doubt as you read it over, your attention will be drawn to those aspects of the record that strike you as important—you are likely to immediately appraise some of the apparent strengths/weaknesses of the record. That's fine. The more intuitive observations and assessments you make, the better.

If you feel in need of some help in analyzing the record, consider asking some of the questions listed here. By the way, you will notice that some of these questions are value-laden. That is my bias showing through. If you don't share the values, don't use the question.

1. *Was the amount of soliciting appropriate?* Given the context of the lesson, did the teacher give enough direction to student activity to keep them productively involved? Or, possibly, was the teacher overbearing to the point of trying to control every move the students made?

2. *To what extent do the solicitations focus on instructional matters? class management? behavior management? officiating or regulating activities?* You are likely to find that the record here corresponds with the one obtained in Clinical Task 9 (Teacher Function).

3. *How do the solicitations define the subject matter?* Teacher solicitations usually indicate what the *real* subject matter of the lesson is. In this case is it: motor skills? game tactics or strategies? routine movement tasks (e.g., an exercise)? ideas, concepts, or principles? attitudes toward sports or toward others? To what extent is the subject matter as revealed in the solicitations similar to or different from what the teacher intended to emphasize?

4. *How do the solicitations shape student involvement in motor tasks?* Are students being asked to replicate a prescribed movement or skill, or to explore alternatives in solving a movement problem and then identify their own solution? Indeed, are students being encouraged to *think* about what they are doing (i.e., engage in "intelligent practice") or merely to do it? Does the teacher ask questions that get the students to analyze and evaluate their own performance, or does he or she provide all the analysis and evaluation?

5. *How do the solicitations shape student involvement with cognitive material (facts, concepts, etc.)?* Does the teacher encourage the students to talk (verbalize) about important movement concepts, strategies, and other ideas related to the subject matter of the class? In fact, does the teacher ask questions that prompt *students* to provide instructional information? And when the teacher does ask such questions, do they merely ask the students to recall specific facts that were stated earlier by the teacher, or to use their own cognitive skills to analyze problems, apply principles, synthesize information, and/or evaluate ideas?

Of course the underlying issue in questions 4 and 5 is: to what extent is the teacher encouraging the students to be independent learners—i.e., to become actively involved in searching out solutions to the problems they encounter and in taking responsibility for assessing their own progress? Most modern theorists advocate a liberal use of indirect teaching methods (discussion, problem solving, guided discovery, and the like) that enable the student to "learn how to learn" and thus become more self-reliant. Do you agree? If so, does this record of solicitations portray a teacher who is intent on producing independent learners?

By the way, for what it's worth, I believe in a balanced mixture of indirect and direct methods. The teacher should certainly encourage students to explore, to analyze, and to reach their own solutions. But the teacher should also lecture, demonstrate, and evaluate student performance. After all, it would be grossly unfair to expect students to rediscover all the accumulated wisdom of human-kind.

The next question bears on this same issue.

6. *How much control is the teacher exercising over the students' activities?* The corollary to this question is: To what extent are the students free to choose what they do? Do the teacher's solicitations narrowly prescribe or allow for some student choice in: which activities the students participate in? where they perform them? how many times they perform them? when the activities begin and end? what the students should attend to when performing? One study of physical education classes indicates that teachers mainly direct students to perform specified activities and rarely encourage students to make their own choices (Hurwitz, 1974).

7. *How do the solicitations shape student involvement with each other?* Do they ask students to: watch each other? talk to each other? assist each other? spot for each other? evaluate each other? cheer for each other? Or, in the absence of such solicitations, is the underlying message that they should have very little to do with each other?

A CLOSER LOOK AT REACTIONS

Teacher reactions to students tell the students what the teacher thinks of their performance, ideas, or general behavior. Often they also reveal how the teacher feels about the students as people. In some instances, teacher reactions serve some very specific purposes—such as providing feedback about a student's motor performance—and can be assessed in terms of how well the purpose is accomplished. In a larger sense, the entire pattern of teacher reactions that occurs during a class period sets the tone for the class and can have an impact that goes beyond the sum of the individual reactions. A case in point is the teacher whose reactions amount to a constant put-down of students and effectively destroy the chances for establishing any sort of positive class atmosphere.

Clinical Task 17 asks you to closely examine teacher reactions in a physical education class. The procedure to be followed is essentially the same as the one used in the previous Clinical Task. In your analysis don't be afraid to read between the lines, to search for the real messages teachers are sending to students, and to assess the impact of the pattern of reactions on class atmosphere.

Clinical Task 17—TEACHER REACTIONS TO STUDENTS

Go through the same procedures you followed in Clinical Task 16, except this time obtain a record of teacher *reactions*. (See Sample Record: Teacher Reactions, p. 86.)

SAMPLE RECORD

TEACHER REACTIONS

CLASS: Fifth grade gymnastics (middle segment of class); approximately 15 min.

NOTES: (S) = Reaction to what student says   TEACHER: Eric Jones

1. "Boy, that was a good one."
2. "OK."
3. "That's good right there." (Students doing monkey rolls)
4. "Some of you are not rolling out in the middle; you scoot across."
5. "That a boy."
6. Begin rocking chair.
7. "That's a little bit better." (sarcastic)
8. "That's not the floor!"
9. "What do you mean 'Oh, gosh!'" (S) (playful tone)
10. "OK." (positive)
11. "OK."
12. "Stay on your mats."
13. "Agghhh — put your knees together." (disgustedly)
14. "There you go — yeah."
15. "That's it."
16. "That's it, that's it, Perkins."
17. "You're bending in the middle, Curly."
18. "I don't want a big guy like you to demonstrate this — I can't even lift you." (S volunteered to assist demonstration; remark made kiddingly)
19. "You're trying to hold him up too long."
20. "That a boy." (enthusiastic)
21. "That's good."
22. "OK."
23. "OK."
24. "Sure he can lift you up."
25. "That a boy — good."
26. "I told you not to touch that." (S disruptive; angry tone)
27. "Jimmy, what's wrong with you!"
28. Students begin headstands.
29. "Ahhh — you people aren't putting your legs next to one another."
30. "Your feet aren't together."
31. "Come on — come on." (sarcastic)
32. "I saw some good headstands and I saw some not-so-good headstands."
33. S started before teacher signal. "Hey, you! I didn't tell you to do anything yet."
34. "That's good."
35. "That's good."
36. "That's good — OK."
37. "Your hands are too far apart."

SUMMARY COMMENTS AND EVALUATION

Did plenty of reacting to student's motor performance. Most of it was positive and general; negative feedback was more specific.

Positive feedback was enthusiastic, but needs to be made more specific; "OK" and "that's good" are overused.

Must be more careful in use of sarcasm; even when I'm kidding with students, some students may be hurt by it.

Should call more of the students by name.

There are virtually no reactions to what students say because there was little opportunity for them to talk. Should I change this?

Only two misbehaviors were reacted to; perhaps one of the reactions was too harsh.

Questions to ask about teacher reactions

Start your analysis of teacher reactions by subjectively appraising the record (as you did with solicitations). Then consider asking selected questions from those listed below.

General questions

1. *Does the teacher react enough? or perhaps too much?* Given the context of the lesson, did the teacher provide a reasonable amount of feedback about students' verbal and motor performance? Did the teacher react enough to indicate that she or he really cares about what the students were doing and about helping them do better?

2. *Are the reactions generally positive, negative, or mixed?* Do the teacher's reactions show support for what students are doing, or for the progress being made? Indeed, do the reactions reveal a positive regard for students as people? Or do they persistently focus on student mistakes, inadequacies, misbehaviors, and so on? Is there a spirit of good humor, playfulness, or enthusiasm in at least some of the reactions? Or is the whole scenario relatively grim and threatening? In case you want to compare this record with the behavior of others, Morgenegg (1978) found that on the average physical education teachers react positively 46%, negatively 22%, and neutrally 32% of the time.

3. *Are the reactions suitably varied or stereotypical?* Is the teacher in a rut? Does she or he repeatedly use the same terms despite wide variations in the situation? For example, are virtually all student performances met with a "good" or "OK"? Or does the teacher display a repertoire of different reactions designed to suit the particular situation or student?

4. *Are the reactions personal or impersonal?* Does the teacher react to individuals? Does he or she use the student's name when addressing an individual? Is there something in the teacher's reaction that indicates she or he knows or cares about Billy, or Linda, or Sue?

Questions about reactions to motor performance (feedback)

1. *Is there an appropriate balance between general and specific feedback?* Does the teacher give general praise and encouragement to appropriately reward deserving performances? Does the teacher give specific praise or specific criticism when needed to reinforce or correct particular aspects of the students' performance? Most teachers tend to give general praise and specific criticism (Tobey, 1974).

2. *Does the feedback come in the form of words or movements?* Most teachers rely exclusively on words to provide students with feedback about their movements (Tobey, 1974). Does this record of teacher reactions show a similar reliance on words? Would it have been more appropriate in some instances to *show* the student what he or she did?

3. *Does the feedback draw the student's attention to crucial aspects of the*

motor skill, and the student's unique performance of it? Study the features of student performance referred to in the teacher's reactions. Do they really zero in on the critical aspects of the skill? Does the teacher seem to provide feedback about the same aspect of the skill, regardless of which student is performing it? If so, is it possible that the teacher is insensitive to individual variations in performance?

4. *Does the feedback explain as well as identify?* Is the teacher merely telling the students what was right or wrong, when it might have been appropriate to explain *why* it was right or wrong? Explanations often contain the ideas that enable students to correct their own performance during future practice.

Questions about reactions to what students say

1. *Was there any?* Our research indicates that physical education teachers rarely react to what students say, largely because students talk very little to the teacher, especially about subject matter (Barrette, 1977). Is this true of the record being analyzed here? If so, how do you feel about it?

If this record of teacher reactions does contain a reasonable amount of reactions to what the students say, examine it more closely. Start by asking selected questions, from those listed previously, that would be applicable here. In addition, you might ask:

2. *Did the teacher's reactions show support for and acceptance of the students' ideas?*

3. *Did the reactions encourage the students to clarify or elaborate on their ideas?*

4. *Did the teacher allow the student enough time to express the ideas fully?*

If you are interested in carefully studying teacher reactions to student talk, I suggest you consult *Discovering New Dimensions in the Teaching Process* by Morine, Spaulding, and Greenberg (1971), or *Classroom Communication Through Self Analysis* by Parsons (1974).

Questions about reactions to other student behavior. Most teachers are concerned about having a reasonably orderly class and so they react to such things as whether the students are following the rules, behaving appropriately toward one another, doing what they are asked to do, going where they are supposed to go, and so on. Broadly speaking, these types of reactions fall under the categories of "behavior management" and "class management." If the record of teacher reactions obtained here includes some of these kinds of reactions, consider the following questions:

1. *Do the teacher's reactions focus on reprimanding misbehavior or on rewarding appropriate behavior?* Most studies of classroom interaction show that teachers concentrate on punishing misbehaviors instead of on rewarding appropriate behaviors, despite the fact that rewards for appropriate behavior have been consistently shown to be more effective in controlling misbehavior (Dunkin and Biddle, 1974). Does this record reveal a tendency to accentuate the negative and

ignore the positive? If so, perhaps the teacher should concentrate more on react-ing to the things students do correctly—this goes for following rules as well as for things like getting organized quickly, paying attention, and so on.

2. *Does the teacher overreact to misbehavior?* Does the teacher constantly stop the class to reprimand students for minor infractions that really would be better to forget about? Does the punishment fit the crime, or is it excessive? Or, on the other hand, is the teacher letting things get out of hand by only sporadi-cally attending to serious behavior problems, or by being oblivious to what's happening?

3. *Is the reaction directed toward the behavior or the student?* Sometimes teacher reprimands can be perceived as attacks on the student as a person, instead of on what he or she did. Needless to say, this could have detrimental long-term consequences for both student and teacher.

4. *Are the reasons for the reaction clear?* Do the target student and other students in the class know why the student is being commended or reprimanded? If not, there's a good chance that nothing will be learned from the incident.

Those who are interested in exploring constructive approaches to class man-agement and discipline should consult Siedentop (1976) for some excellent sug-gestions.

INTERACTIONS WITH INDIVIDUALS

A teacher's interactions with an individual student can have a powerful im-pact on the student. (On second thought, "individual student" is the wrong term, I really mean Steve Miller, Marilyn Harris, Marvin Wilson, real people.) One serious interchange between you and Arthur Jones can make him feel a lot better about himself. One traumatic blow-up between you and Stacy Martin can make her despise you for weeks. Over time, a *pattern* of discouraging interactions between you and Alice Smith can destroy her attitude toward gym, just as a series of supportive interactions between you and Brad Thomas can rekindle his interest in physical activities. In the absence of any attention from you, Shirley Simon may give up.

In the previous Clinical Tasks we've focused on the patterns of your inter-actions as they are spread across all of the students in your class. In Clinical Task 18, the focus will be on how you interact with Johnny, with Karen, with Philip, with any others. First, you will be asked to record another teacher's interactions with individuals, then have someone record these interactions in a class you teach. (Of course, if you have a videotape of your class, you can analyze it.) The focus for the observation is on *teacher interactions with individual students*— i.e., those instances when a teacher is communicating with one student. Disre-gard all other teacher interactions directed toward the whole class, or toward a group of students.

It may not be easy to find an observer who knows the names of the students in your class. If you are a student teacher, the cooperating teacher would be the logical choice. In an elementary school setting, the classroom teacher might be enlisted to assist. However, if there is no qualified observer immediately available, consider a compromise; have someone learn the names of ten or fifteen students in your class on one day, and then return on the following day to code your interactions with those ten or fifteen.

You might want to vary the procedure to focus on your interactions with certain individuals, instead of covering all individual interactions will all class members. Perhaps you want to concentrate on your interactions with a couple of problem students, a shy student, a hyperactive child, a low achiever, a star, your pet, and so on. If so, pick out four or five or more students and have the observer record only your interactions with them. Having done so, however, recognize that, given your prior knowledge of which interactions are to be recorded, you may not behave "normally" toward those students.

Clinical Task 18—INTERACTIONS WITH INDIVIDUALS

1. Observe a class taught by another teacher, one in which you know the names of the students. *Each time the teacher interacts with an individual student*, write a brief summary of the interaction (see Sample Record, p. 91). When possible, record key words or phrases used by the teacher so you can capture the flavor of the interchange. Note the initials of the student with whom the teacher is interacting next to each summary. If you know only some of the students in the class, record only those interactions with the students you know.
2. Show the record to the teacher who taught the class and, together with the teacher, make appropriate entries under Summary Comments and Evaluation. Review the Questions to Ask about Interaction with Individuals and use them selectively in your analysis of the record.
3. Have someone keep a record of your interactions with individuals as you teach a class, then complete step 2. Or, if you have a videotape of your own teaching, use it for the analysis.

SAMPLE RECORD

INTERACTIONS WITH INDIVIDUALS

CLASS: <u>Station Activities (stunts, tumbling, other) 4th Grade</u> TEACHER: <u>Howard Tompkins</u>

CODES: S = Student; T = Teacher; MJ, JP, etc. = Student's initials

1. Extended personal conversation. — MJ	15. S falls off beam—teacher spends much time talking to her and checking for injury. — FR
2. "Can't you get here on time?" — JP	
3. "I love those sneakers." (sarcastic) — JP	16. "Nice, Cheryl. That was your best one yet." (S on mats) — CT
4. "Anne, please get over where you belong." — AG	17. "This is the last time I'm going to warn you, Joey." (S is pushing another student) — JP
5. Asks S to help him with the mat. — RF	
6. Instructs S on leg cuts on horse and compliments S on performance. — TS	18. "Do you have the right hand position? That's better, much better." — BM
7. After S does forward role, T puts arm around his shoulder; tells him how much he is improving. — BM	19. "Ted, you have to wait until she's off." (balance beam) — TS
8. "Keep your hands apart." — CC	20. "Do you know where you are supposed to be?" (said harshly) — AG
9. "Hey, you know you're not allowed on the horse now." — JP	21. "Stay on the mat." (tumbling) — SB
10. "OK, that's good." (S on beam) — ST	22. "Go over there and sit down until I tell you you can come back." (S was fighting) — JP
11. Spots S on bars and compliments "very, very good." — TF	
12. S asks if he can play basketball. T says "No." S asks "Why?" T says "Because I said so." — LM	23. "OK, OK Sue." (floor exercise) — SP
	24. Teacher asks Mary to help Alice with headstand. — MJ
13. S asks to be spotted on handspring. T spends time spotting her and gives several compliments. — MJ	25. "Come on Billy, try it." (cartwheel) "OK, OK you'll get it next time." — BM
	26. "That's terrific Mary." (round off) — MJ
14. Spots S on round off; gives corrective feedback; asks S to try again, says "Good." — RK	27. Tells Joey he can participate now only if "he behaves himself." — JP

SUMMARY COMMENTS AND EVALUATION

Mary (MJ) is one of my favorites, she got a lot of my attention, as usual — perhaps too much.

Billy (BM) has a learning disability, lacks coordination, is reluctant to participate. I'm pleased to see I gave him the attention and encouragement he needs.

Joey (JP) is a big problem, constantly misbehaving. I'm always yelling at him or punishing him. Personally I don't like him. But something has to be done to change the way I relate to him.

Anne (AG) is a bit fuzzy, never seems to get directions straight, but there is absolutely no reason for me to be abrupt with her.

Overall, I interacted with 15 different students out of the 27 enrolled in the class, that seems reasonable.

I meant to get around to Alice and Timmy. They need a lot of help in gymnastics, but I forgot.

Questions to ask about interactions with individuals

The main concern of this analysis should be to find out *how* you are relating to different individuals; *why* you are relating to someone in a particular way; and *whether you should* attempt to change things.

Start by searching the record for students with whom you've had several interactions, enough to have established a pattern of interaction. Target those students for analysis. Also, search for crucial interactions which in your judgment might have had an important influence on the student. Target the students in those interactions for analysis.

Recognize that there are likely to be numerous routine or mundane interactions that are not significant enough to bother with any further. Don't try to analyze every single interchange that took place.

Having targeted some students for further analysis, examine your interactions with each one, and for each student consider asking some of the following general questions.

1. Is the record of your interactions with Sue typical of the way you normally interact with her? If not, you may want to give less attention to this part of the record.
2. How are you treating Sue? Try to characterize the way you are relating to her.
3. If you were Sue, how would you characterize the way the teacher is treating you?
4. Are you treating Sue the way you *want* to treat her? Are you treating her the way you *should* treat her?
5. By the way, who is Sue? What kind of person is she? Is there anything about her that suggests she should be treated in special ways?
6. Do you like her?
7. *Why* are you interacting with her in the way you do?
8. Would it be advisable to change the way you interact with her? Given the circumstances, is it possible to make the change?

There is a limitless variety of other more specific questions that you might ask. Let me suggest a few that reflect my own biases. Does the record indicate that:

You care about her?

You are interested in her as a person?

You support her efforts?

You understand and accept her weaknesses?

You are actively engaged in trying to help her progress?

After you've analyzed the interactions between yourself and these target students, consider the other students. Which names are missing from the records? Would some of the missing names also be missing from similar records of subsequent classes? Why?

MAKING CHANGES

By now you should be familiar with the procedure for making changes in teaching based on records obtained from class observation and analysis. Use the records obtained in Clinical Tasks 15, 16, 17, and 18 to determine which if any changes should be made, plan for the changes, teach, and evaluate whether or not they were made. (See Clinical Task 19.)

Don't be too ambitious. Your records of interactions are likely to be extensive, and you may see numerous things that need to be changed. Pick out one or two changes and concentrate on making those first; then if you have the energy, try some others.

Also, realize that compiling verbatim records of solicitations and reactions can be burdensome; devise a simpler method of recording whether the changes were made. For example, suppose you are interested in increasing the number of times you give specific/positive feedback to students. Simply have someone observe you and record a check (✔) each time you give that type of feedback. Or perhaps you would like to increase opportunities for students to identify concepts that underlie effective performance. Simply have an observer note each time you ask a question that calls for that type of student response.

Clinical Task 19—CHANGING TEACHER-STUDENT INTERACTIONS

1. Review the records, comments, and evaluations from Clinical Tasks 15, 16, 17, and 18. Identify the *one* or *two* most important changes you believe should be made in your teaching performance.
2. Plan to incorporate those changes in a subsequent class.
3. Teach the class and have an observer record the extent to which the changes were made. Have the observer use a simplified notation system to verify the changes.
4. Analyze the results, and, if you wish, move on to making other changes.

FOR THE ENTHUSIAST

You enthusiasts (assuming there are still some of you left out there) probably have noticed that we left considerable ground uncovered in these analyses of teacher-student interaction. For example, we *didn't* "take a closer look" at teacher responses, student solicitations, student responses, or student reactions. Feel free to do so.

Furthermore, we didn't carefully examine the relationships between certain sets of moves such as teacher solicitations and student responses; student responses and teacher reactions to those responses; or the complete cycle of teacher solicitation–student response–teacher reaction. You might examine those relationships with an eye toward answering such questions as: Are the students responding appropriately to teacher requests? Is the teacher reacting appropriately to the student's response?

The possibilities for further examination of these interactions are really boundless. If some other feature of student-teacher interaction strikes you as being crucial, by all means pursue it. By this time you should have acquired a repertoire of approaches to observation and analysis that will enable you to design an appropriate data-gathering technique for whatever you want to examine.

Other forms of interaction analysis

As mentioned earlier, there are numerous systems for analyzing interaction between teachers and students. Certainly the most popular of these systems has been Flander's (1970) *interaction analysis system.* The original version of the system consisted of the following ten categories for coding teacher and student talk in classroom discussions: "Teacher talk: 1. accepts feeling, 2. praises or encourages, 3. accepts or uses ideas of pupils, 4. asks questions, 5. lecturing, 6. giving directions, 7. criticizing or justifying authority, 8. pupil talk—initiation, 9. pupil talk—response, 10. silence or confusion." The system was designed to reveal the prevailing climate in the classroom by determining the pattern of directness versus indirectness of the teacher's behavior. Since its inception the system has been revised many times by various researchers. Daugherty (1971) and Cheffers (1974) have developed adaptations of interaction analysis suitable for use in physical education classes. If you have the time, try to locate a copy of the interaction analysis system and at least read about it. If it looks promising, perhaps you might use it. I'd suggest that you start by using the original version to code a class discussion (i.e., an extended verbal interchange) between teacher and students.

7

Putting the pieces together: a picture of your own teaching

You have amassed an enormous amount of information about your own teaching in the process of completing the preceding Clinical Tasks. Records of all types abound. They stem from a sequential and detailed examination of component parts of the teaching process, each part having a somewhat limited and distinct focus. Sometimes the total picture that emerges from this sort of piecemeal examination is not altogether clear. Most of the pieces may be there, but it may not be easy to see how they fit together. In effect, although you have accumulated a vast store of knowledge about your teaching, it may be difficult to integrate that knowledge into a coherent view of your status and progress as a teacher. What I hope to do in this chapter is to help you to fit some of the pieces together so you can see more clearly where you are, and figure out where to go from here in terms of your own teaching.

YOUR CONCEPT OF TEACHING

One way to start putting the pieces together is to clarify your concept of teaching, and then use that concept to reexamine and reorganize the information you have already collected.

The term "concept of teaching" is used broadly to refer to the array of ideas and beliefs you have about teaching, particularly those ideas that reflect what you think teaching *should* be. Concepts of teaching take a range of forms depending on the values, preferences, past experiences, and knowledge of the individuals who formulate them; most people, however, focus primarily on the essential *goals of teaching* and the *critical processes* required to reach those goals.

Most of us already have a concept of teaching (ill-defined though it may be). We carry it with us in our heads and use it occasionally to plan and carry out teaching decisions. More often than not, however, the concept is vague. We are not sure about where we stand on certain issues, or why we do some of the things we do. Indeed, we sometimes act out of habit or follow routines without regard for our fundamental beliefs. Developing a concept of teaching is in part a matter of clarifying and organizing those somewhat ill-defined ideas that have been used all along to guide our teaching.

Your past work in the analysis of teaching is replete with important ideas from your own concept of teaching. Consider all of the evaluative judgments you've made, the criteria you've developed, the objectives you've set for students, and the intentional changes you've made in your teaching; all of these are based on underlying ideas and beliefs that together constitute a sizable portion of your concept of teaching. Of course, at the moment these ideas appear in disparate segments of your work and consequently may seem unrelated. Formulating your own concept of teaching will in part involve gathering these underlying ideas and fitting them together in a coherent pattern.

The development of an "informed" concept of teaching should extend beyond personal introspection; it should rely in part on outside resources. Consulting authoritative publications, research evidence, the views of colleagues and supervisors, student opinion, and curriculum guides can expand your concept to encompass previously overlooked elements. It can also help to ensure against the development of a narrow-minded and short-sighted concept. I hope you will have the time and the inclination to consult some of these resources as you work out your concept. In case you are not sure about where to start, let me suggest a few resources in physical education that have been useful to me in working out my own concept of teaching: (1) Mosston's (1966) spectrum of styles is still one of the most thought-provoking conceptions of teaching; (2) Siedentop (1976) views teaching with an emphasis on skill in classroom management and interpersonal relations; (3) Singer and Dick (1974) offer a detailed description of the systems approach to teaching; (4) Heitmann and Kneer (1976) focus on individualized instructional techniques; and (5) Cassidy and Stratton (1974) concentrate on the humanistic aspects of the teacher's role.

Reflective Task 1 asks you to clarify your concept of teaching by outlining what you believe are the *most important goals* of teaching, and the *most crucial functions* teachers should carry out to reach those goals. By all means, don't try to write down all of your ideas—you'll never finish. Select those that, in your judgment, are most vital. Then try to organize them in a logical manner so that the relationships among ideas are apparent. A few illustrative ideas based on concepts formulated by other teachers appear in the Sample Analysis (pp. 100-103); they may provide some useful hints about possible approaches to the organization of your own ideas.

Use whatever resources are available to you in completing the task. Let me offer a few suggestions.

1. Review past records of completed Clinical Tasks, particularly those sections dealing with your own Evaluations and Comments.
2. Talk to colleagues/supervisors/professors; get their reactions to your ideas.

3. Review key portions of books or articles that you've read about teaching; selectively incorporate those ideas which fit in well with your own.
4. If the school district in which you are working has a viable curriculum guide or teachers' handbook, see if it has anything to offer.

While it's helpful to use outside sources to some extent, make sure the concept you outline is *your own*. It should reflect *your* values, *your* beliefs, *your* preferences, and *your own* current understanding of what teaching is all about. Only a personalized conception of teaching will provide a meaningful basis for continuing your work in the analysis of teaching. Of course, if you are working under a supervisor who evaluates you according to a prescribed set of criteria or you are enrolled in a course in which the professor expects you to adopt his or her ideas about teaching, it may be prudent to make sure that your concept coincides with theirs—or perhaps you would prefer to be more daring.

In any event, make sure you *write down* your ideas. With something as complicated as a concept of teaching, you condemn yourself to eternal fuzziness if you try to keep it all in your head. Also, as you put your ideas on paper, recognize that they constitute a transient statement of your position; the ideas will change with time, provided you don't stagnate.

Reflective Task 1—OUTLINING YOUR CONCEPT OF TEACHING

Develop a written outline that depicts your concept of teaching. Include in it: (1) the most important *goals* of teaching; and (2) the most crucial *functions* teachers should perform to achieve these goals. The concept can be related to teaching in general, or to teaching in your own particular school setting.

USING YOUR CONCEPT OF TEACHING TO ANALYZE THE RECORDS OF YOUR TEACHING

Once you have outlined your concept of teaching, it should provide a useful framework for reexamining and organizing the information you've been collecting about your teaching. Reflective Task 2 asks you to match up the information you've been collecting with the various aspects of your concept of teaching. Analyze the match/mismatch, and decide what you might do in the future. The Sample Analysis (pp. 100-103) illustrates the kind of format that might be used in completing this task. Needless to say, since your concept of teaching is likely to differ markedly from the items listed in the Sample Analysis, the contents of your analysis will be substantially different from the example presented.

Reflective Task 2—USING YOUR CONCEPT OF TEACHING TO ANALYZE THE RECORDS OF YOUR TEACHING

1. Review your records of previous Clinical Tasks that provide information about your own teaching. Identify those records that provide important information relevant to particular aspects of your concept of teaching (see Sample Analysis, pp. 101-103). Important information that is not directly relevant to an aspect of your concept of teaching should be listed separately.
2. Analyze the relationship between the information collected and your concept of teaching (see column 2 of Sample Analysis).
    a. Is the record of your performance consistent with your concept?
    b. Have the changes you've made in your teaching produced a closer match between your performance and your concept?
    c. Is more information needed?
    d. If there is no information related to a particular aspect of your concept, would it be advisable to collect such information?
    e. Should your concept of teaching be revised (enlarged) to include aspects that deal with other important information?
3. Identify those things you might do in the future that are suggested by the analysis (see column 3 of Sample Analysis).

If the analysis is completed with some degree of proficiency, there should be several valuable payoffs. First, you should understand better how some of the information you've been collecting fits together—the picture of teaching revealed in the accumulated data should be more organized and coherent in terms of your own ideas about teaching. Second, you should be able to see more clearly whether you are doing what you believe in—i.e., whether the records of your performance as a teacher are consistent with your concept of teaching. Third, you will be able to identify those important aspects of your concept of teaching for which little or no information has been collected.

The insights obtained from this analysis will have some obvious implications for your future work. (1) Having identified some important discrepancies between your concept of teaching and your actual teaching performance, you may try to alter your performance to bring it into closer alignment with your beliefs. (2) Or, having discovered that certain features of your concept of teaching are not realistic, you may choose to revise your concept to make it more consistent with reality. (3) Recognizing that you have not as yet collected any clinical information about some important aspects of teaching (identified in your concept), you might attempt to collect such information in future analyses.

SAMPLE ANALYSIS: ANALYZING PAST RECORDS IN TERMS OF A CONCEPT OF TEACHING

Concept of teaching	Analysis of relevant information	Future plans
Goal: Facilitate student learning of motor skills.	(Task 13: Evaluating Students) Above-average and superior students showed adequate gains. Other students showed little or no gain.	Devise strategies to improve performance of below-average students.
Related functions		
1. Provide appropriate amount of expert instruction, using variety of instructional techniques.	1. (Task 9: Teacher Function) One-half of my time spent in giving instruction (Task 11: Instructional Content) Key aspects of skills are covered. (Task 14: Evaluation of Instruction) Preparatory instruction was too drawn out, at times unclear; students had to wait too long to get involved; I relied too much on verbal communication—demonstration and visual aids rarely used. (Task 12: Change in Teacher Behavior) Improved frequency of demonstration.	1. Make preparatory instructions more concise, integrate instruction with practice.
2. Provide adequate opportunity for students to practice skills.	2. (Tasks 5 and 6: Coding Student Behavior) Students spend less than 12% of time practicing skills, game settings provide little practice for low achievers. (Task 7: Change) Some improvement made in expanding practice opportunities (16%), more expansion needed.	2. Continue to work for more optimal amounts of student practice. Arrange game settings to provide more practice for low achievers.
3. Diagnose individual student learning problems and provide corrective as well as reinforcing feedback.	3. (Task 10: Direction of Teacher Behavior; Task 17: Teacher Reactions) Frequent feedback provided to individual students, most of it tends to be positive and general. (Task 14: Evaluation of Instruction) Diagnosis of student errors in volleyball was poor; many errors overlooked and no corrective feedback given.	3. Work on diagnosis of skill errors and providing appropriate corrective feedback.
4. Vary the learning tasks to suit different levels of student ability.	4. (Task 2: Informal Analysis by Colleague; Task 14: Evaluation of Instruction) Virtually all students perform the same tasks regardless of ability. (Task 4: Informal Analysis by Students) Some students believe tasks are too easy and repetitious, others feel tasks are too demanding.	4. Arrange learning tasks in order of progressive difficulty; allow for individualized rate of progress.

Goal: Promote student enjoyment and satisfaction in motor activities.

(Task 2: Informal Self-Analysis) I thought students enjoyed most classes. (Task 4: Student Informal Analysis) Student reactions to classes were mixed; many of the more poorly skilled students are apparently not having fun. "Enjoyment" and "satisfaction" are not easy to measure or estimate. More information is needed here.

Conduct informal student analysis to find out more about *why* they do or do not enjoy certain activities. Try to determine what behaviors reflect enjoyment and satisfaction, and systematically search for the presence of these behaviors in classes.

Related functions

1. Provide adequate time for participation in recreational games and activities.
2. Provide positive reinforcement for student involvement in activity.
3. Show personal (teacher) enthusiasm for the activities and for the class as a whole.

1. (Tasks 5, 6, and 7: Coding Student Behavior) Students usually spend less than 9% of their time in game situations, while excessive amounts of time were spent getting organized and waiting around.
2. (Task 2: Teacher Reactions) I react frequently and positively to students.
3. Limited information available on this function. (Task 4: Student Informal Analysis) Some students regard me as being too "serious" and "up-tight."

1. Expand opportunities for student participation through more efficient organization.
2. Keep it up.
3. Discuss this matter with colleague; have colleague observe and provide informal feedback.

Continued.

SAMPLE ANALYSIS: ANALYZING PAST RECORDS IN TERMS OF A CONCEPT OF TEACHING—cont'd

Concept of teaching	Analysis of relevant information	Future plans
Goal: Develop independence and responsibility in students.	No data have been collected that indicate actual degree to which students achieve independence/responsibility.	Is it possible to collect valid data on this goal?
Related functions		
1. Use teaching methods that encourage students to take responsibility for their own learning (e.g., problem-solving, reciprocal teaching).	1. (Tasks 16 and 17: Teacher-Student Interaction) Learning is teacher directed; teacher's directions to students dominate the interactive process. (Task 19: Change in Interaction) Some increase in indirect teaching was noted.	1. Continue to work on development of more indirect teaching methods. Obtain informal feedback from teachers and students as to their effectiveness.
2. Allow students to choose and organize their own activities (periodically).	2. No information collected on degree to which students choose and organize their own activities. My recollections suggest that they do very little of this.	2. Do an objective analysis of the extent to which students in my classes are able to choose activities.
3. Provide for student learning of underlying concepts that will enable them to understand skills, strategies, etc., and thus be able to direct their own learning.	3. (Task 11: Instructional Content; Tasks 16 and 17: Teacher-Student Interaction) Available data indicate little or no focus on underlying concepts; I essentially tell students what to do with minimal attention to explanations of underlying reasons.	3. Plan and teach lessons which include focusing on underlying concepts.

Goal: Provide an orderly and safe class environment.

Related functions

	(Task 14 Supplement: Evaluation of Managerial Functions) In general I was rated high in matters related to class control and safety.	
1. Establish rules for acceptable student behavior and control misbehavior.	1. (Task 2: Informal Self-Analysis) Rules were posted and gone over thoroughly. (Task 14 Supplement: Evaluation of Managerial Functions) Received high ratings for control of student behavior. (Task 9: Teacher Functions) Minimal amount of class time (1%) required to handle behavior problems, indicating low incidence of student misbehavior. (Task 2: Teacher Reactions) The few instances of misbehavior were handled with firm reprimand; in many instances positive behavior control techniques were used.	1. Continue using these methods.
2. Provide well-defined organizational structure for class.	2. (Task 1: Informal Analysis by Colleague) comments indicate class was highly structured, students know where to go and what to do. (Task 7: Spot Check of Student Behavior) Percentage of students engaging in off-task behavior is minimal (3%). (Task 9: Teacher Function) Both students and I spend considerable amount of time getting organized.	2. Continue the well-defined structure, but try to spend less time getting organized.
3. Regulate activities to ensure student safety.	3. (Task 1: Informal Analysis by Colleague) Comments indicate that student safety was provided for. More information needed here.	3. Develop checklist for assessing provisions made for student safety. Have supervisor use it to rate my classes.
4. Check equipment and structure environment for safety.	4. No information has been collected on these items; but my informal recollections are that I have been neglectful here.	4. Add appropriate items to safety checklist (see above).

OTHER INFORMATION NOT CURRENTLY RELATED TO MY CONCEPT OF TEACHING

Analysis of relevant information	Future plans
1. Task 15: Analysis of Teacher-Student Interaction) My manner of interacting with students is not only direct, it tends to be impersonal, serious, and very business-like. I don't like this image that is being conveyed, but I'm not sure what to do about it, or whether it has anything to do with effective teaching.	1. Obtain videotape of a typical sample of my teaching behavior; see if I like what I see. Discuss the matter with colleagues.
2. (Task 4: Informal Analysis by Students) Several students revealed disconcerting attitudes toward the gym classes: "afraid" of activities; "embarrassed" about their physical appearance in class; and "humiliated" by their inept performance. These are very serious personal problems that need attention.	2. Hold individual meetings with troubled students; try to find out why they feel the way they do and how I might help. Revise my concept of teaching to include elements related to personal image, and to students' attitudes toward gym.
3. (Task 18: Interactions with Individuals) I need to pay more attention to shy students of average ability like Ted, Ellen, and Ken. I've tended to ignore them in the past.	3. Periodically recheck my interactions with individuals.

8

Evaluating the match between plans and reality

In most schools teaching is a planned activity—at least it should be. Educators formulate plans that normally include such things as objectives, methods, class organization, resources, and so on. The plans may be highly specific "lesson" plans, more generic unit plans, and/or entire curriculum plans. In most instances the plans are written down, although it must be acknowledged that many experienced teachers manage to avoid writing out daily lesson plans, preferring instead to rely on their memory or instincts. Regardless of the form they take, teaching plans represent our considered judgments as to what should happen in class and what outcomes should accrue. Formulated in advance, at times when calmness, rationality, and reflective thought can prevail, these plans serve as intelligent prescriptions for the hectic realities of interactive teaching.

One of the most useful ways to evaluate teaching is to assess the match between a teacher's plans and the realities that occur in his or her class—i.e., to use the teacher's own plans as the primary basis for making judgments about the efficacy of what happens. One virtue of this approach is that it enables you to tie the evaluation very closely to specific events of the class, instead of trying to use more universal criteria that may not be directly applicable. Another virtue is that the assessment is based on the teacher's own value system, and thus reduces the possibility of making unfair judgments based on values that the teacher does not share, a possibility that is all too often overlooked by some evaluators. Of course, this approach has its limitations as well; the evaluation can only be as good as the original plan on which it is based. An ill-conceived lesson plan will lead to an ill-conceived evaluation.

Clinical Task 20 asks you to plan a lesson, use the lesson plan as the basis for designing an evaluation procedure, teach the lesson, and use the evaluation procedure to assess the match between the plan and what actually happened. This approach marks a transition in your work in the analysis of teaching. In past Clinical Tasks the focus was on a particular analytic/evaluative approach and the development of your ability to use that approach. Now that you have mastered an array of approaches, this task calls on you to use those acquired abilities to create or shape your own approach to evaluation. Here, you start with a comprehensive lesson plan and design the evaluation to fit the particular features of the lesson. The evaluation is now subordinate to your teaching plans. In this respect Task 20 is a model for your future work in the analysis of teaching.

Clinical Task 20—PLANNING, TEACHING, AND EVALUATING THE MATCH

1. Develop a written *lesson plan* for an upcoming class that you will teach. (See Developing a Lesson Plan, below.)
2. In advance of actually teaching the lesson, develop a written *plan for evaluating* the match between your lesson plan and what will actually occur during the lesson. (See Developing an Evaluation Plan, p. 107.)
3. Teach the lesson* and use the Evaluation Plan to collect information and make the required assessments.
4. Examine the evaluative data and determine the match between your plans and what actually happened. Identify any changes that should be made in teaching similar lessons in the future.

---

*If videotape equipment is available, consider the possibility of videotaping the lesson so that you can evaluate your own teaching.

DEVELOPING A LESSON PLAN

There are a number of different ways to construct a lesson plan. At this stage in your teaching you have probably adopted a particular approach to lesson planning that fits well with your philosophy of physical education, with the requirements of your school district or supervisor, and with your own style of teaching. In completing Task 20 develop a lesson plan that is consistent with your normal approach to planning. For example, if you are comfortable with a detailed plan, make it detailed. If you prefer less detail, make it more general. Plan a single lesson for one class period, or generate a plan for a series of lessons. Whatever you do, make sure the plan is *personally useful* as a guide to your teaching. Don't create a monstrosity that will have to be aborted or disregarded.

Furthermore, make this a *personally meaningful* lesson—i.e., one that is designed to achieve goals that *you* consider vital, and uses methods that *you* especially value. To ensure this sort of meaningfulness, perhaps you should review your concept of teaching (Reflective Task 1) and develop a lesson plan that reflects at least some of the crucial features of that concept.

Of course it is also advisable to plan a lesson that fits in with the ongoing program at your school. A lesson plan is, after all, a small piece of a much larger plan called a curriculum. Design this lesson as an integral part of the ongoing curricular sequence.

Having encouraged you to pursue your normal approach to planning, let me also offer a few general suggestions regarding basic ingredients for the lesson plan(s), ingredients that should help to make the plan(s) more amenable for use as a basis for evaluation.

Objectives for students

Clearly specify what students are supposed to know and be able to do as a consequence of the lesson(s). When appropriate, distinguish between cognitive, affective, and motor performance objectives. Make sure the objectives are stated with sufficient clarity and specificity to lend themselves to some reasonable form of assessment. Your previous experience with Clinical Task 13 should be helpful here.

Pattern of activity

Identify the sequence of events or activities for the lesson. What will the teacher do? What will the students do? What pattern of teacher-student inter-action will occur? How will the class be organized? What teaching methods or strategies will be employed?

Special features

Identify any crucial features of the lesson that for some reason deserve special attention—possibly the behavior of certain students, or the use of a particular teaching aid, or the efficiency of certain administrative procedures, etc.

If you feel that you need more guidance in planning lessons, you might begin by consulting Gagne and Briggs (1974), Mager (1975), Siedentop (1976), or Singer and Dick (1974).

DEVELOPING AN EVALUATION PLAN

The major concern in devising the evaluation plan is to be certain that the evaluation will determine whether the lesson plan was implemented—i.e., whether what happens matches the lesson plan. There are basically two types of matches to assess: (1) whether the lesson's objectives were accomplished, which normally involves the evaluation of those student behaviors which reflect the accomplishment of objectives; and (2) whether the planned pattern of activity actually occurred, which usually requires collecting information about ongoing events and determining whether they coincide with the plan. In assessing the match, you might select previously used methods of evaluation, revise previous methods, combine methods, or create an entirely new method—choose whatever method best determines the match between plans and reality.

The most serious mistake made by teachers completing this task is to choose evaluative methods which for one reason or another they like, but which have no earthly relationship to the important features of the lesson plan. Try to avoid this pitfall.

Keep the evaluation plan simple. Choose one, two, or at most three of the most crucial features of the lesson to evaluate, and collect data only on those features. You already know how complicated the analysis and evaluation of teaching can be. Don't try to investigate all of the complexities at once.

Be sure to develop the evaluative plan *before* you teach the lesson. In this way you commit yourself in advance to evaluating those features of the lesson which your best judgment indicates are most crucial, and you are likely to choose methods of evaluation that constitute a fair test of whether the lesson plan was implemented. On the other hand, if you wait until after the lesson has been taught to develop some or all of the methods of evaluation, you may fall victim to the enticing tendency to evaluate only those things that you already know worked best.

Of course, in developing the evaluative plan carefully consider what is (or is not) *feasible* in your school setting. If, for example, you don't have a colleague or supervisor who is willing to observe the class, or if you have uncooperative students who won't fill out assessment forms, obviously you'll have to design an evaluative procedure that takes account of these limitations. In some instances this may mean that you are forced to abandon a superior evaluative approach in favor of a less effective but manageable one. So be it.

Listed here is a series of questions designed to guide the development of an appropriate evaluative plan, accompanied by some suggestions. Sample lesson plans, together with their corresponding evaluative plans, appear on pp. 110-112.

- Did the students achieve the planned performance objectives? Consider using:

  A performance measure (Task 13)

  An informal appraisal of student performance by a colleague/supervisor (Task 2)

- Did the students achieve the planned cognitive objectives? Consider using:

  A knowledge test (Task 13)

- Did the students achieve the planned affective objectives? Consider using:

  Informal feedback from students (Task 4)

  A measure of change in student attitude (Task 13)

- Were the major features of the planned "pattern of activity" implemented? Consider using:

Informal appraisal by a colleague/supervisor who uses the lesson plan to guide observation (adaptation of Task 1)

Informal self-analysis regarding whether plan was implemented (Task 2)

- Did the teacher's behavior follow the planned "pattern of activity"? Consider using:

Coding of appropriate dimensions of teacher behavior (Tasks 9, 10, 11) by colleague or supervisor

Your own system for coding aspects of teacher behavior specified in the plan and have colleague/supervisor use it

- Did the students' behavior follow the planned "pattern of activity"? Consider using:

Coding of appropriate aspects of student behavior (Tasks 5, 6, 7) by colleague or supervisor

Your own system for coding aspects of student behavior specified in the plan and have colleague or supervisor use it

- Did the pattern of teacher-student interaction occur as planned? Consider using:

Coding of teacher-student interaction (Tasks 15 through 18) by colleague

Your own system for coding aspects of interaction specified in the plan and have a colleague/supervisor use it

- Was the quality of teacher behavior consistent with the standards implicit in the plan? Consider using:

Direct evaluation of teacher behavior (Task 14) by colleague/supervisor

- Were teaching methods or strategies implemented as planned?

Select or develop an evaluative/analytic procedure to detect whether the particular method or strategy was employed and then use it.

- Were the "special features" implemented as planned?

Select or develop an evaluative procedure appropriate to the particular special feature. (Possibly use variation of direct evaluation, Task 14.)

INTERPRETING MATCHES AND MISMATCHES

As a general rule you expect things to go as planned. Since your lesson plans represent your best judgment as to what should happen, there will be a natural tendency to be pleased when reality matches your plans and to be disheartened when there is a mismatch, so the "matches" will receive positive evaluations and the "mismatches" will be evaluated negatively. That's as it should be, most of the time—but not always. There are times when unfolding events in class signify the need for a change of plan in midstream. A teacher who is tuned in to such signals is likely to digress from his or her original plan. In such cases the record will show a mismatch. Is that bad? There are times when unfolding events in class signify the need for a change of plan but the teacher is *not* tuned in to such signals, and so he or she plows ahead as originally planned. (Some teachers who *are* tuned in plow ahead anyway.) Such behavior will produce a record that shows a close match with the original plan. Is that good?

Sometimes, in the midst of a lesson you come up with a brilliant idea that you hadn't thought of before. You try it out and it works. So you continue to pursue it and in the process abandon your original intentions. The lesson turns out to be a smashing success. The record shows an enormous mismatch. So?

Some people struggle to follow their plan, but are incapable of doing so largely because of their own lack of skill in teaching. They end up with a record of glaring mismatches. But, cleverly, they invent a host of reasons that justify what they did—so they explain away the mismatch. Is that good?

Interpreting matches and mismatches can be a tricky business. Be careful.

SAMPLE EVALUATION

Lesson plan (batting)	Evaluation plan	Evaluative data
Objectives for students		
1. Utilize proper form and technique in hitting softball.	Evaluate this at later time.	
2. Enjoy and engage enthusiastically in batting practice game.	Use informal written feedback from students to determine their enjoyment and enthusiasm for batting practice game.	Eighteen of the twenty-two students indicated they preferred this type of practice to other types we used. Twenty of twenty-two students described practice as "enjoyable" or "fun."
Pattern of activity		
(Previous lessons involved instructions in basics of batting)		
1. Organize class into four groups for batting practice. One student leader in each group serves as assistant teacher.	Teacher informally evaluates instruction given by student leaders.	In general, student leaders gave incorrect instruction and other students did not take them seriously.
Teacher circulates among groups, diagnoses problem, and provides corrective feedback. Concentrates on four major aspects of technique: 1. Grip 2. Stance 3. Eye on ball 4. Follow-through	Observer codes teacher references to major aspects of technique and rates teacher's diagnosis of student performance.	Teacher neglected to focus on "grip," "stance," and "follow-through." Instead concentrated on "eye on ball" and "point of contact" with ball. Teacher rated "good" to "excellent" on most diagnoses of student performance.

SAMPLE EVALUATION—cont'd

Lesson plan (batting)	Evaluation plan	Evaluative data
Pattern of activity—cont'd		
2. Organize batting practice game. Each of four groups bat/field simultaneously in four different areas. Objective is for each group to obtain maximum number of "successful" hits into designated area within 5-minute games. Rotate batters every minute.	Collect informal written feedback on student enjoyment (see above).	Incidental observation: two hitting areas overlapped, made for dangerous setting.
Special feature		
This is teacher's first attempt at use of assistant teacher.	Teacher informally evaluates assistant teacher (see above).	

Summary evaluation and comments

1. The students enjoyed the batting practice game as planned, but batting areas need to be rearranged to reduce danger of being hit by batted ball.
2. Teacher did not emphasize four aspects of technique as planned, but aspects that were emphasized were more crucial. Change future plans to focus on "point of contact."
3. Assistant teachers were useless; reexamine this entire method.

SAMPLE EVALUATION

Lesson plan (bump pass)	Evaluation plan	Evaluative data
Objectives for students		
1. Demonstrate initial proficiency in using the volleyball bump pass.	Observer counts ratio of successful to unsuccessful bump passes during modified volleyball game at end of period.	Success ratio, 39%.
2. Accurately identify appropriate "principles of application of force" as they relate to proper execution of the bump pass.	No time to evaluate this.	
Pattern of activity		
1. Students engage in volleyball games (six teams), focus on practice of previously learned skills. Teacher circulates and gives instructional feedback (10 minutes).	Observer, using copy of lesson plan, times duration of each major segment of the lesson.	Observed durations: (1) games, 9 minutes; (2) large group instruction, 12 minutes; (3) paired practice, 7 minutes; (4) modified game, 8 minutes.
2. Large group instruction. Teacher introduces bump pass, explains and demonstrates how to execute it. Explains principles of "application of force" as they relate to proper execution (7 minutes).		Large group instruction took much more time than planned, detracted from time available for modified game.
3. Students pair up and practice bump pass with partner. Teacher circulates and provides instructional feedback (8 minutes).	Observer codes number of practice trials completed for two different pairs of students, focusing on one pair for first half of practice, then on the other pair for the second half. Multiply results by 2.	Pair 1, 62 practice trials per child; pair 2, 26 practice trials per child. Number of practice trials was more than expected.
4. Students play modified volleyball games using only bump pass. Substitutes rotate into game. Teacher circulates and provides instructional feedback (12 minutes).	Observer codes ratio of successful to unsuccessful passes during game (see above).	
Special features		
1. Keep large group instruction time short to maintain high level of student motivation.	See results (above).	
2. Provide concentrated skill practice in pairs to compensate for reduced opportunities for practice during game.	See results (above).	

SAMPLE EVALUATION—cont'd

Summary evaluation and comments

1. There was an adequate match between "initial proficiency" objective and student performance. Measure progress in performance in subsequent lessons. In future collect information regarding knowledge objective.
2. Plan for concentrated practice (in pairs) worked well; use it in other classes.
3. Did not follow the time allocation plan; large group instruction took too long; students were bored. In future plan to cover less material and/or integrate instruction with practice.

SAMPLE EVALUATION

Lesson plan (explore/balance)	Evaluation plan	Evaluative data
Objectives for students		
1. Explore and use various bases of support in maintaining balance on balance beam.		
2. Discover which bases of support provide greater/lesser stability and why.	Teacher conducts small group (4 students) discussion at end of period. Asks questions that test whether students have discovered which types of supports provide greater/lesser stability, and whether they know why.	Only one of the four students was able to answer any of the questions correctly. None was able to give adequate explanations of why.
Pattern of activity		
Class organized into four groups which rotate to different activity areas: (1) balance beam, (2) balancing tasks on mats, (3) partner work on balancing, (4) exploratory movements over and under obstacles.	First half of period, observer spot-checks students at each activity area, records on-task/off-task.	The percentage of students on-task at each station was: balance beam, 95%; balance task (mats), 86%; partner work, 46%; exploratory movements, 67%.
Teacher is stationed at balance beam. Spots students. Uses guided discovery technique to encourage student discovery of which basis of support yields greater stability and why. Teacher solicits solutions from students, does not provide solutions.	Second half of period, observer codes teacher solicitations, student verbal responses, teacher reactions (and notes when teacher provides answers to problem).	Teacher solicited only three correct verbal responses (solutions) from students. Teacher reacted by giving solutions twenty-three times.
Special feature		
1. React positively to John Crawford's on-task behavior periodically throughout class.	Observer notes reactions.	Number of positive reactions, 5.

Summary evaluation and comments

1. Guided discovery technique was not used as planned; much additional practice with this technique is needed.
2. The students did not discover which bases of support provide stability; perhaps this was due in part to the inept use of guided discovery.
3. Students in unsupervised activity areas were on-task a sufficient proportion of the time, except for partner work. There was too much fooling around between partners.
4. John was reacted to as planned.

9

Reflections and prospects for the future

COMPLEXITY IN TEACHING

This text opened with some observations about the complexity of teaching. It's time to return to that topic.

Teaching always has been and always will be a complicated business. Our appreciation of that complexity, however, may change dramatically over time. What we once viewed in relatively simplistic ways, may come to be recognized for all its intricacies, especially when it is the subject of concentrated study and analysis. This kind of emerging appreciation for the complexity of teaching is a common by-product of completing the Clinical Tasks.

Now you contemplate a slice of teaching (perhaps 5 minutes of class time) and recognize that:

It contains continuous streams of events; a different stream for each participant; for teacher, for Johnny, for Dana, for Susan, for Jackie, etc.

The behavior of each participant constantly changes, as does the context in which it occurs

Each behavior has an intent, a duration, a mode, a quality, an effect, a tone

The behaviors are entangled in networks of mutually influential actions and reactions

The whole pattern of activity is related to a plan for the class; a plan that is/is not being implemented to some degree at various points in time

Each overt behavior is only a part of the individual's experience; much goes on below the surface

And then there are the outcomes, the residue of it all; the ways in which people have changed as a consequence of the experience

Such expanded awareness of the complexities of teaching has value, if for no other reason than it allows for a truer perception of reality. It has other virtues as well. For example, you will be more likely to study a teaching situation carefully before making judgments and decisions. (For you, the days of quick observations and snap judgments are probably a thing of the past.) When you do make judgments, they will be made with a fuller appreciation of the evidence on which they are based. Indeed, you will be ever so cognizant of what you *don't know* about a

115

teacher, a student, a situation, a class, etc. Awareness breeds modesty, and modesty is certainly a virtue. Isn't it?

Of course, "there will be times when you may be so awed by the complexities of a teaching situation that you find it difficult to make a decision and to act," at which point you will probably yearn for a return to simpler days when you blissfully forged ahead, unencumbered by the inherent intricacies you faced. When this happens, don't be dismayed; it's quite natural to be hesitant in a maze. To borrow a phrase from Arthur Miller, "It comes with the territory."

YOUR COMPETENCE IN THE ANALYSIS OF TEACHING

While you may not feel like the world's foremost expert in the analysis of teaching at this moment, don't underestimate the repertoire of analytic methods you now have at your disposal, methods in which you've developed at least initial levels of proficiency. You can objectively code student behavior, teacher behavior, teacher-student interaction. You know how to classify that behavior in terms of its intent, direction, mode, and content. You've learned to vary sampling procedures by coding within fixed time intervals, recording the frequency of events, spot-checking, and so on. You've developed techniques for assessing teaching in terms of its impact on students. You know how to establish criteria and use them as the basis for collecting evidence about teaching quality. You can combine and invent analytic methods to determine whether teaching plans are being implemented. You are familiar with a variety of ways for using others to assist in the analysis of your teaching, particularly your own students. You've had considerable practice in interpreting and appraising evidence collected, then using that appraisal to plan and carry out changes. "

Equally important, you've come to know the strengths, weaknesses, and limitations of these methods. For example, you recognize the fragmentary nature of the evidence yielded by any method. You can distinguish between objective and subjective evidence. You understand that it is one thing to appraise the teaching process as it occurs, and quite another thing to appraise its impact on student learning. You know the only way to obtain an accurate record of what students do is to watch them one at a time—but to generalize from one student's behavior to the behavior of the class is, at best, a risky business. You are aware of the fact that most evaluative judgments reflect the biases of the observer, and that the usefulness of those judgments hinges on the competence of the observer and the nature of those biases.

Having this repertoire of methods and knowing their strengths and weaknesses puts you in a position to make intelligent choices about which methods to use in the future.

FUTURE USE OF ANALYSIS

By now your feelings about analyzing teaching are well established. You may have become a zealous proponent of analysis, convinced of its indispensable value to your continued professional development, and eager to make it a regular part of your teaching. (We authors thrive on such optimistic and hopelessly naive expectations.) Or, you may have mixed feelings about the whole business, recognizing that some techniques have value at certain times, while others do not; in which case you might be open to the occasional use of selected analytic techniques in the future. Or you may be so delighted at being finished with what you have found to be a relatively worthless enterprise that you are not likely to return to it. Whatever your feelings, there's nothing more that I can do to change them at this stage of the game.

Let's assume, however, that you are moderately enthusiastic about the value of analysis and are ready to use it, at least occasionally, in the future. Where do you go from here? Let me offer a few suggestions.

Take it easy and make it fun

In all probability you've had to complete the Clinical Tasks within a fixed time period. As a consequence the work has been concentrated and at times onerous. Now you are free to proceed at a more leisurely pace and to use techniques that you like. Do the kinds of analyses you've enjoyed doing in the past and do a small piece at a time. If you don't have fun analyzing teaching, you'll soon abandon it.

Pursue your own interests

You have some firm convictions and ideas about the crucial constituents of teaching (see your Concept of Teaching). You've analyzed your own teaching in terms of these ideas and identified things that need to be done in the future. By all means, pursue some of those plans. They represent *your* values and priorities; they must be important.

Analyze the implementation of your plans

Clinical Task 20 was intended to serve as a model for future analysis. Basically, it is a flexible approach that allows you to determine whether you are doing what you intend to do. Consider using simplified variations of it to pursue your own interests.

Consider extending the focus from lessons to units

In learning the analytic techniques we have focused on a lesson, or a class, or even part of a class. Consider extending the focus to an instructional unit. Some techniques can be easily adapted for use in evaluating a unit. For example, evaluate student performance at the beginning, middle, and end of a unit; collect informal or structured feedback from students at the end of a unit; have someone code student or teacher behavior at strategic points in the unit. In effect, use an approach similar to Clinical Task 20, only instead of using the lesson plan as the basis for evaluation, use the unit plan.

Evaluation of an entire curriculum is a massive undertaking. It involves entire teaching staffs and an elaborate array of data-gathering procedures. If such an evaluation is contemplated in your school, consider the ways in which the analytic techniques you've learned might be used to contribute to the project. An assessment of a sample of lessons and units is a fundamental part of any well-designed curriculum evaluation.

Keep records

You've already amassed a substantial set of records of your teaching. It would be a shame if they were tucked away in the back of some drawer and never again saw the light of day. After all, they are an important historical commentary on your teaching. They document the status of your performance and aspirations during an important stage in your professional development. How about organizing the records and putting them in the front of the drawer so you can refer to them from time to time? Organize them in a way that makes sense for you: perhaps by grade level, or by activity, or according to important features of your teaching, or by the analytic technique used.

Once you've started a record file, why not continue to maintain it? As you engage in analyses in the future, file the records appropriately. Such records not only keep you in touch with where you've been, they provide the basis for current decision-making. Consider, for example, the utility of having records of student reactions to an extensive variety of activities over a 2- or 3-year period; or perhaps having evidence of the degree of student progress in certain activity units from year to year; or a record of the teaching strategies that worked and those that failed over time. History can certainly help us to intelligently plan for the future, provided there is a reasonably accurate historical record to compensate for our otherwise notoriously faulty memories.

Don't be a loner

After studying the social realities of teaching, Lieberman and Miller (1978) conclude that teachers are "private" about teaching. They normally "do not share experiences about their teaching, their classes, their students, or their perception of their roles with anyone inside the school building." My own experience confirms this observation. Unquestionably, such isolation impedes professional development. It is exceedingly difficult to maintain motivation and interest in teaching if there is no one to talk to about what you are doing. One of the underlying goals of this book has been to break down the barriers of privacy by encouraging mutual involvement in Clinical Tasks.

It is virtually impossible to continue to pursue your interest in the analysis of teaching alone. You'll have to overcome the normal tendency toward privacy and get someone else involved with you, someone who not only can serve as observer or coder or evaluator, but someone with whom you can discuss results, problems, plans, successes, and disappointments. A physical educator teaching in your school would be an ideal colleague in this undertaking, or possibly a classroom teacher, or a supervisor, or a student teacher. Convince someone to work with you; otherwise you'll soon get tired of talking to yourself and quit.

References

Anderson, W. G. *Teacher behavior in physical education classes,* Part I: Development of a descriptive system. Unpublished manuscript, Teachers College, Columbia University, 1974.

Anderson, W. G., and Barrette, G. T. (Eds.). *What's going on in gym? Descriptive studies of physical education classes.* (A special monograph of Motor Skills: Theory into Practice. Newtown, Conn.) 1978.

Barclay, R. *Critical incidents in the instruction of beginning swimming.* Unpublished doctoral dissertation, Teachers College, Columbia University, 1968.

Barrette, G. T. *A descriptive analysis of teacher behavior in physical education classes.* Unpublished doctoral dissertation, Teachers College, Columbia University, 1977.

Bellack, A. A., Davitz, J. R., Kliebard, H. M., and Hyman, R. T. *The language of the classroom.* New York: The Institute of Psychological Research, Teachers College, Columbia University, 1966.

Bickman, L. Data collection 1: observational methods. In *Research methods in social relations,* 3rd ed. New York: Holt, Rinehart and Winston, 1976.

Boehm, A. E., and Weinberg, R. A. *The classroom observer: a guide for developing observation skills.* New York: Teachers College Press, 1977.

Cassidy, R., and Stratton, F. C. *Humanizing physical education: methods for the secondary school movement program.* Dubuque, Iowa: Wm. C. Brown Publishers, 1974.

Cheffers, J. T. F., Amidon, E. J., and Rodgers, K. D. *Interaction analysis: an application to nonverbal activity.* Minneapolis: Association for Productive Teaching, 1974.

Cheffers, J. T. F., and Mancini, V. H. Teacher-student interaction. In *What's going on in gym? Descriptive studies of physical education classes.* (A special monograph of Motor Skills: Theory into Practice. Newtown, Conn.) 1978.

Costello, J. A. *A descriptive analysis of student behavior in elementary school physical education classes.* Unpublished doctoral dissertation, Teachers College, Columbia University, 1977.

Costello, J. A., and Laubach, S. A. Student behavior. In *What's going on in gym? Descriptive studies of physical education classes.* (A special monograph of Motor Skills: Theory into Practice. Newtown, Conn.) 1978.

Daugherty, N. A plan for analysis of teacher-pupil interaction in physical education, *Quest,* 1971, *15,* 35-50.

Dunkin, M. J., and Biddle, B. J. *The study of teaching.* New York: Holt, Rinehart and Winston, 1974.

Fishman, S. E. *A procedure for recording augmented feedback in physical education classes.* Unpublished doctoral dissertation, Teachers College, Columbia University, 1974.

Fishman, S. E., and Tobey, C. Augmented feedback. In *What's going on in gym? Descriptive studies of physical education classes.* (A special monograph of Motor Skills: Theory into Practice. Newtown, Conn.) 1978.

Flanagan, J. C. The critical incident technique, *Psychological Bulletin,* 1954, *51,* 327-358.

Flanders, N. A. *Analyzing teaching behavior.* Reading, Mass.: Addison Wesley Publishing Co., 1970.

Gagne, R. M., and Briggs, L. J. *Principles of instructional design.* New York: Holt, Rinehart and Winston, 1974.

Garis, R. *Critical incidents in the instruction of gymnastic activities for girls.* Unpublished doctoral dissertation, Teachers College, Columbia University, 1964.

Gibson, J. G. *A study of effective and ineffective behaviors of college supervisors of student teaching in physical education.* Unpublished doctoral dissertation, Teachers College, Columbia University, 1969.

Hall, R. V. *Managing behavior: Part I.* Meriam, Kansas: H & H Enterprises, 1970.

Heitmann, H. H., and Kneer, M. E. *Physical education instructional techniques: an individualized humanistic approach.* Englewood Cliffs, N.J.: Prentice-Hall, Inc., 1976.

Hurwitz, R. F. *A system to describe certain aspects of the physical education teacher's role in the learning activity selection process.* Unpublished doctoral dissertation, Teachers College, Columbia University, 1974.

Laubach, S. A. *The development of a system for coding student behavior in physical education classes.* Unpublished doctoral dissertation, Teachers College, Columbia University, 1975.

Lieberman, A., and Miller, L. The social realities of teaching, *Teachers College Record,* 1978, *80,* 54-68.

Mager, R. F. *Preparing instructional objectives,* 2nd ed. Belmont, Calif.: Fearon Publishers, Inc., 1975.

Morgenegg, B. L. *The pedagogical functions of physical education teachers.* Unpublished doctoral dissertation, Teachers College, Columbia University, 1977.

Morgenegg, B. L. Pedagogical moves. In *What's going on in gym? Descriptive studies of physical education classes.* (A special monograph of Motor Skills: Theory into Practice. Newtown, Conn.) 1978.

Morine, G., Spaulding, R. S., and Greenberg, S. *Discovering new dimensions in the teaching process.* Scranton: International Textbook Company, 1971.

Mosston, M. *Teaching physical education.* Columbus, Ohio: Charles E. Merrill, 1966.

Parsons, T. W. *Achieving classroom communication through self-analysis.* El Segundo, Calif.: Prismatica International Inc., 1974.

Peck, R. F., and Tucker, J. A. Research on teacher education. In R. M. W. Travers (Ed.). *Second handbook of research on teaching.* Chicago: Rand-McNally Publishing Co., 1973.

Siedentop, D. *Developing teaching skills in physical education.* Boston: Houghton Mifflin Co., 1976.

Simon, A., and Boyer, E. G. (Eds.). *Mirrors of behavior,* II. Philadelphia: Research for Better Schools Inc., 1970.

Singer, R., and Dick, W. *Teaching physical education: a systems approach.* Boston: Houghton Mifflin Co., 1974.

Tobey, C. *A descriptive analysis of the occurrences of augmented feedback in physical education classes.* Unpublished doctoral dissertation, Teachers College, Columbia University, 1974.

Index